AWAKENING
TO YOUR
MULTIDIMENSIONAL
SELF

Harnessing Energy, Timelines, and
Higher Consciousness

Lisa Thompson, PhD

Awakening to Your Multidimensional Self: Harnessing Energy, Timelines, and Higher Consciousness

www.DrLisaJThompson.com
ISBN: 979-8-9918968-8-7

Book Design by Transcendent Publishing
Author Portrait by: Ilana Maxwell
Edited by Mary Rembert

Printed in the United States of America.

"You are more energy than you are physical.
You are powerful creators, and the more you play
with raising your vibration, the more you will experience
true joy and unity with all."

—Arcturian Uluru channeled by Lisa Thompson,
Connection to the Cosmos

CONTENTS

DEDICATION

To my Galactic Family, whose boundless love inspires me to live authentically, courageously, and with wonder. This journey—and these pages—are a tribute to the cosmic connection we share.

ACKNOWLEDGMENTS

This body of work would not have been possible without the unwavering love and support of my late husband, Skip Thompson. When I decided to make a huge timeline shift and step into the world of my spiritual business, he was right there by my side, cheering me on every step of the way. Even as I transitioned into my Galactic mission—a path he didn't fully understand—he remained my biggest fan, always encouraging me to embrace my full, authentic self. His love and belief in me have left an indelible mark on my heart and soul, and I carry him with me in everything I do.

I am deeply grateful to my friend and mentor, Sunny Dawn Johnston, who has been a constant source of guidance and inspiration for the past seven years. Her wisdom has supported me in both my personal life and my business journey. Sunny exemplifies what it means to live a high-vibrational life, and I am honored to have her by my side.

To my friends and loved ones, who continue to grow and evolve with me and who accept me for exactly who and what I am—I am grateful beyond words. You know who you are, and your love and acceptance mean the world to me. Thank you for walking this path with me.

I am incredibly thankful to my Arcturian family, who first connected with me in 2018. Their continuous reminder to me—and to all of humanity—that we have the power to choose which timeline we want to be a part of has been a profound source of inspiration for this book. They are the catalyst for this creation, and I am deeply honored to share their wisdom.

SECTION I

Understanding
Your Multidimensional Self

CHAPTER 1

CHOOSING YOUR TIMELINE: THE KEY TO SPIRITUAL ASCENSION

"In every moment, the universe is creating infinite possibilities in our lives. We only need to align our thoughts and intentions to step into the reality we desire."

—Deepak Chopra

Imagine if you could consciously choose your timeline, shifting into the reality that aligns with your highest potential and deepest desires. What would that look like for you? At the quantum level, all timelines exist simultaneously. There is no past and no future, only the eternal now. This understanding breaks open the illusion of linear time that has shaped much of our human experience. What if every decision, thought, and intention shifted you into a new timeline? What if the timeline you didn't choose still exists, waiting for another version of you to live it out?

Timelines are like infinite pieces of paper stacked on top of each other. Each piece represents a different version of reality. You can jump between them and do so all the time, often without realizing it. Every choice you make alters your trajectory, aligning you with a new reality. The magic happens when you become conscious of this process and understand that what you focus on creates your reality.

In this chapter, I will share my personal journey of timeline shifts and how they opened me to the Galactic Realm and my role as a Galactic Ambassador. I invite you to explore how to consciously choose your timeline, release what no longer serves you, and step fully into your multidimensional nature.

My Timeline Shift Into the Galactic Realm

When I was 15, I had an experience that changed my life forever. I was living on 20 acres in Yelm, Washington, and it was late fall. Like any other night, I went to bed, snuggling with my stuffed animal, Mr. Floppytail, a platypus that had become a source of comfort over the years. Little did I know that when I woke up, I would find myself in a different reality—a timeline that would reveal to me that there is far more to life than the third-dimensional experience we know.

I awoke inside a spacecraft. The interior was small, like a shuttle, with just me and my extraterrestrial (ET) guide inside. Strangely, I wasn't afraid. He appeared human, and I had an inexplicable sense of familiarity as though I had met him before. The walls of the craft seemed transparent, allowing me to see the vastness of space surrounding us. As we flew through the solar system, I asked him telepathically where we were headed. He told me we were traveling to Io, one of Jupiter's moons. What unfolded next shifted my understanding of reality.

Inside the moon, I saw what appeared to be a hospital facility, with humans being examined in various rooms. When I asked my guide if he was human, he revealed that he and others there were not human, but humanoid. They disguised themselves to avoid frightening the humans brought to their facility. He explained that those of us brought to Io were being tested—to see if we could survive in environments like this if something catastrophic happened on Earth. It was 1988, during the Cold War, when the threat of nuclear conflict and global destruction was real. There was a timeline where Earth faced such devastation, and we were being prepared for it.

This was the first timeline shift I became consciously aware of. But it wasn't until much later that I began to fully explore the depths of our multidimensional nature.

Realizing Our Multidimensional Nature

Over seven years ago, I was called to study past life regression work. This training opened my eyes to how deeply interconnected our timelines and lifetimes are. I began to experience different realities firsthand— timelines in which I had lived other lives, played other roles, and existed in other dimensions. This understanding led me to the realization that we are multidimensional beings, existing simultaneously across different timelines and realities.

A year after my regression training, I took a class in psychic intuition. During a meditative journey, I encountered a group of blue-skinned beings. They radiated a message of love and unity: "You are one of us. We are one of you. We are family." This was my first conscious connection with the Arcturians, a highly evolved extraterrestrial race that I would come to understand as part of my soul family. From this point on, my journey into the Galactic Realm expanded.

My interactions with these higher dimensional beings—whether the Arcturians or other galactic races—helped me understand that we are much more than this one Earth life. We are multidimensional energies, and our experiences stretch far beyond what we perceive with our physical senses. This revelation changed how I viewed life and my purpose.

A Dramatic Timeline Shift

In September 2023, my life took a turn that would shift me into an even greater timeline. My husband, Skip, took his life suddenly and dramatically. It was a shock to my entire being, especially as I was in the middle of leading one of my Galactic Retreats.

The morning after discovering his body, I sought answers from nature. Speaking to the trees outside the condo where I was staying, I received a clear message: To be on my path of highest ascension, there had to be a massive timeline shift where Skip couldn't move forward with me.

Although Skip had loved and supported me, he didn't fully understand the depth of my galactic work. He shared with me after his passing that he could support me more from the other side than in the physical, and he encouraged me to continue my mission. This experience shifted me in profound ways. I let go of the desire to be "normal" or fit into society. I fully embraced my Galactic Ambassador role and the multidimensional nature of my being.

What If We Could Choose Our Timeline?

Reflecting on my own experiences, I've come to believe that our ability to choose our timeline is the secret key to spiritual ascension. Every thought, every decision, and every belief is an opportunity to shift into a new timeline. What if you could consciously choose the timeline where you live in your highest potential, aligned with love, joy, and unity? What if you could let go of the stories and limitations that keep you stuck in the past and step fully into your power?

You can. You already are. By reading these words, you have chosen a timeline where we are here together, co-creating this reality. The key is to understand that you have the power to shift at any moment. The timelines you didn't choose still exist, but by consciously focusing on your highest vision and aligning with the energy of love and abundance, you move into the reality where that vision is your lived experience.

Releasing What No Longer Serves You

To shift into your desired timeline, you must be willing to let go of what no longer serves you. This includes old stories, limiting beliefs, and relationships that aren't aligned with your new frequency. As you raise your vibration and step into a higher timeline, some people, places, and things will naturally fall away. This is part of the ascension process.

Let go of old stories—The stories you tell yourself about who you are and what is possible for you are often rooted in past experiences that no longer align with your highest self. These stories keep you anchored in lower timelines. It's time to release them and create new narratives based on your expanded understanding of who you truly are.

Release relationships that no longer resonate—As you shift into higher timelines, you may find that some relationships no longer fit. These people may not understand your growth or resonate with your new frequency. It's important to let them go with love and gratitude, knowing that you are making space for new connections that align with your highest self.

Stepping Into Your Light and Power

Now is the time to fully step into your light and power. You are a multi-dimensional being, and you can choose your timeline to create a reality that reflects your highest potential. The higher dimensional extraterrestrials I've connected with want humanity to understand that we are so much more than this one Earth life. It's time to join our galactic family, to live in the energy of love and unity, and to fully embrace the truth of who we are.

This journey is about spiritual ascension, about moving into higher frequencies where love, compassion, and joy are the dominant experiences. As you raise your vibration and consciously choose your timeline, you become a beacon of light, helping others do the same.

I invite you to join me on this expansive journey. Together, we can co-create a new reality that reflects the highest potential of humanity and the universe.

What timeline will you choose?

CHAPTER 2

THE QUANTUM NATURE OF TIME AND THE POWER OF CHOICE

Reality, as we perceive it, is much more fluid and expansive than the traditional understanding of time as a straight line moving from past to future. At the quantum level, all timelines exist simultaneously, transforming our perception of life and allowing us to rethink the past, present, and future. Understanding how consciousness shapes reality allows us to see how every decision aligns us with a specific timeline. With this awareness, we can consciously shape the reality we desire through the power of choice.

The Illusion of Linear Time

For most of human history, time has been understood as a linear progression—a continuous stream from the past to the future, with the present moment being the only point where we can act. We think of time as a sequence of "before" and "after," where cause and effect unfold predictably. This view has influenced how we structure our lives, make decisions, and understand our personal journeys.

While this perception of time helps navigate daily life, it oversimplifies a far more dynamic and complex reality. Quantum mechanics, the study of particles at the smallest levels of existence, reveals that time does not behave as a strict sequence of events. Instead, time is an interconnected web of possibilities, with multiple outcomes existing simultaneously. In this framework, time is less like a linear path and more like a field of potential that you can tap into and influence with your thoughts, choices, and actions.

The Quantum Nature of Time

In the quantum realm, particles exist in a state of superposition, meaning they occupy multiple potential states at once until they are observed. This discovery suggests that all possible outcomes coexist in the present moment, awaiting your conscious awareness to collapse them into a singular reality. The act of observation itself is what brings one potential reality into focus, turning possibility into actual experience.

This principle is often illustrated by the double-slit experiment, in which particles (like photons or electrons) behave like waves when unobserved, spreading out and existing in all possible states simultaneously. However, once these particles are observed, they behave like particles, choosing a single path. The conclusion is that observation and consciousness play a role in determining reality.

Superposition and Human Experience

If particles exist in superposition, occupying all possible states simultaneously, what does this mean for your life? Every decision you make can be thought of as creating a branching path that leads to infinite potential realities. Much like particles, you exist in a state of quantum superposition—all potential versions of your life exist at once. You experience only one timeline based on your choices and focus.

Imagine standing at a crossroads, with each direction representing a different version of reality. Your choice determines which timeline you step into, while the other paths remain unchosen potentials. Although you may only perceive one version of reality, the other potential outcomes still exist in parallel, subtly influencing the possibilities available to you in the future. The key to understanding time and reality at the quantum level is recognizing that time is not linear—it is fluid, and your perception of time is shaped by where you direct your awareness.

This realization leads to an important conclusion: You are not bound by the past nor limited by an inevitable future. The only reality that truly matters is the one you are aware of right now. In the quantum universe, the past is not fixed, and the future is not predetermined. Every moment is a point of infinite potential, and you can change the course of your life at any moment by shifting your focus and making new choices.

The Stacked Timeline Metaphor

To further understand the concept of nonlinear time, imagine infinite pieces of paper stacked on each other. Each piece represents a different timeline—a potential version of reality. Some timelines are similar, while others are drastically different. These sheets all exist at once, and as a conscious being, you are constantly moving between them based on the choices you make and the thoughts you focus on.

This metaphor is not just illustrative but aligns with certain interpretations of quantum theory. Time doesn't flow from one moment to the next in a linear fashion, like a river. Instead, all moments exist simultaneously, much like the pages of a book. Your consciousness acts like a reader, flipping through these pages and choosing which timelines to experience by where you place your attention.

Each timeline contains a different set of circumstances and experiences. Every time you make a decision, no matter how small, you are choosing which timeline to inhabit. For example, if you decide to take a certain job, you move into a timeline where that choice shapes your future. However, the other timelines—where you made different decisions—continue to exist, but your awareness has shifted to the timeline you are currently experiencing.

The Power of Conscious Choice

In the quantum world, observation collapses potential into reality. This means that your focus and attention directly influence which timeline you experience. Your thoughts, beliefs, and emotions are not passive forces; they actively shape your reality by aligning you with certain possibilities within the quantum field.

Consider your mind as a radio tuner, adjusting its frequency to match the timeline you experience. If you focus on what you want to achieve, your energy aligns with timelines where those desires are more likely to manifest. On the other hand, if you focus on fear or doubt, you tune into a timeline where those experiences become more prominent.

The Observer Effect

The concept of the observer effect plays a crucial role here. The observer effect refers to the idea that the act of observation affects the outcome of an event. This principle is demonstrated in the double-slit experiment, where particles act as waves when unobserved but behave as particles when observed. The observation seems to collapse the wave of possibilities into a single reality.

This effect applies to how we interact with reality daily. If you consistently focus on negative outcomes or dwell on your fears, you are more likely to align with timelines where those fears come true. However, if you focus on positive outcomes, gratitude, and what you truly desire, you actively influence your reality to reflect those possibilities.

Conscious Choice in Daily Life

Every decision, no matter how small, shifts you into a different timeline. The thoughts you entertain, the actions you take, and the emotions you feel all determine which version of reality you experience. You are not a passive observer in life but a conscious creator.

Imagine waking up each morning and choosing how you want your day to unfold. You decide to focus on positivity, abundance, and opportunity, and as a result, you align with timelines where those qualities dominate your experience. Conversely, if you start the day feeling stressed or fearful, you align with timelines where those emotions shape your reality.

The power of conscious choice is fundamental to navigating the quantum nature of time. You are always at a decision point. By focusing on what you want rather than what you fear, you consciously shift into a timeline that reflects your highest desires. This skill can be cultivated through mindfulness, intention, and awareness.

Shaping Your Reality Through Focus

Since your thoughts and attention collapse potential into reality, it's essential to understand that what you focus on expands. This means that if you focus on the challenges and difficulties in your life, they are likely to multiply. But if you focus on solutions, opportunities, and abundance, those experiences will expand in your reality.

Let's take a practical example: You're considering starting a new business, but fear of failure looms large. If you focus on the possibility of failing, you will likely align with a timeline where obstacles and setbacks hinder your progress. But if you shift your focus to envisioning success, creative solutions, and opportunities, you align with a timeline where those possibilities are more likely to manifest.

The Relationship Between Choice and Vibration

Vibration plays a key role in the timeline you experience. Everything in the universe operates at a specific frequency, including your thoughts, emotions, and beliefs. Your personal frequency, or vibration, attracts experiences that match that same frequency.

If you're vibrating at the frequency of gratitude, joy, and abundance, you attract experiences that reflect those qualities. However, if your vibration is aligned with fear, worry, or lack, you attract experiences that mirror those lower frequencies. By choosing thoughts and emotions that raise your vibration, you can consciously shift into higher timelines that reflect your highest potential.

Becoming a Conscious Creator

Understanding the quantum nature of time and the power of conscious choice empowers you to take control of your life in profound ways. You are no longer bound by a rigid, linear perception of time or limited by past decisions. Instead, you are a conscious creator, capable of shifting between timelines and creating the reality that aligns with your highest potential.

Every moment is a decision point where you can choose the reality you want to experience. By focusing on what you want, aligning your vibration with your desires, and making empowered choices, you can step into a timeline that reflects your greatest aspirations. As you continue to practice this awareness, you will experience greater freedom, fulfillment, and alignment with your true self.

In upcoming chapters, we will explore how you can apply this understanding to navigate between timelines more effectively. By shifting your focus, aligning with your highest desires, and making empowered choices, you can step into a reality that reflects your deepest aspirations and fulfills your soul's purpose.

In the next chapter, we will explore the polarized reality of third- and fourth-dimensional frequency and how to overcome fear and judgment.

CHAPTER 3

POLARITY—GETTING OVER THE FEAR AND JUDGMENT THAT HOLDS US BACK

Polarity is a fundamental aspect of the human experience on Earth. It's the mechanism through which we, as multidimensional beings, evolve and expand. But what is polarity, and why do we experience it?

We constantly shift between third-, fourth-, and fifth-dimensional frequency vibrations. In the third and fourth dimensions, we experience third density, which is characterized by duality—the constant push and pull between opposing forces such as good and bad, light and dark, positive and negative.

This duality is part of our polarized experience on Earth, where we engage in a wide range of emotions, beliefs, and situations that reflect this split. As we ascend into fifth-dimensional frequency—a higher vibration of love and unity—we enter fourth density, where the concept of duality fades, and we start to experience a more unified, harmonious reality.

In this chapter, we will explore how polarity shows up in our lives, why it's an essential part of our spiritual evolution, and how to overcome the fear and judgment that polarity often brings. Understanding polarity from a higher perspective allows us to release the need for judgment, transcend our limitations, and live from a place of compassion, acceptance, and love.

The Purpose of Polarity in Human Experience

As Earth humans, we experience polarity as part of our journey through third density. It's a tool for growth, a way to explore the full range of emotions, roles, and experiences that help us evolve and expand our consciousness. Polarity allows us to see both sides of every situation and engage with duality to learn, grow, and ultimately move beyond it.

The roles we play—In this polarized reality, we take on different roles in relation to others—sometimes we are the hero, and other times we are the villain. These roles are not inherently good or bad; they are simply opportunities to experience different aspects of life and gain wisdom. We may find ourselves judging others for their actions or judging ourselves for the roles we play, but this judgment is part of the illusion of duality.

Polarity as evolution—Polarity is not meant to trap us in suffering. It's a mechanism of evolution, designed to help us learn through contrast. By experiencing both joy and pain, love and fear, empowerment and disempowerment, we come to understand the full spectrum of human emotion. This, in turn, helps us to grow spiritually and feed that knowledge back to Source.

Soul contracts and life lessons—Before we incarnate on Earth, we make soul contracts—agreements with other souls to play certain roles in each other's lives. We choose our parents, friends, and even our so-called enemies. We do this to learn specific lessons and experience the full range of polarity. These relationships are not random; they are carefully planned by our higher selves to help us evolve.

My Personal Experience of Polarity

One of the most profound experiences of polarity in my life came through my first marriage. It was a highly volatile relationship, marked by abuse and disempowerment, which I later came to understand as a victim-tyrant dynamic. At the time, I felt trapped, unworthy, and unable to escape the situation. But looking back from a higher perspective, I now realize that this experience was part of a larger soul contract that I had agreed to before incarnating.

When I first met my husband, I felt an instant soul recognition. I had a vision of a past life in Scotland during the time of William Wallace, where we had been together. This gave me insight into why we had come together again in this life—to complete a story and learn important lessons.

During our marriage, I experienced verbal, emotional, and mental abuse, and there were moments of physical violence as well. I convinced myself that I was unworthy of love and accepted this treatment for the sake of our business and other people's investments. It wasn't until the birth of our daughter that I found the courage to leave the relationship and shift into a new timeline.

Eighteen years after leaving the marriage, I can now look back with a deep understanding and compassion. I chose this experience to fully understand what it means to feel disempowered and to learn how to reclaim my power. I have forgiven myself for staying in the relationship and have forgiven my ex-husband for his role in it. I now understand that he was playing his part in our soul contract, helping me to evolve.

Judgment: A Reflection of Ourselves

One of the primary ways that polarity shows up in our lives is through judgment—judgment of ourselves and others. We are trained in this polarized reality to categorize things as good or bad, right or wrong. This leads to judging people who are different from us and judging ourselves when we don't meet certain expectations or standards.

When we judge others, it's often because they reflect something within us that we have not yet healed. For example, if we judge someone for their behavior or beliefs, we are likely projecting our unresolved emotions onto them. All judgment is a mirror, showing us where we need to heal.

We are often our harshest critics, judging ourselves for our perceived failures, shortcomings, or mistakes. This self-judgment keeps us trapped in lower vibrational states, preventing us from fully stepping into our power. When we heal the judgment within ourselves, we can release the judgment we place on others.

What would happen if you could release all judgment? Could you accept yourself and others exactly as they are without trying to change or control them? This is the key to overcoming polarity. When we release judgment, we create space for compassion, understanding, and acceptance, allowing us to rise above the duality of good and bad.

Healing the Wounds of Self-Judgment

Much of the judgment we project onto others stems from our unresolved wounds. Where do you judge yourself? This judgment often manifests as feelings of guilt, shame, or inadequacy. We compare ourselves to others and find ourselves lacking, or we feel superior to others in an attempt to validate our worth. These judgments result from conditioning in a polarized world, where we've been taught to measure ourselves against external standards.

Self-judgment can take many forms, contributing to a cycle of negativity and self-condemnation. These forms of self-judgment often manifest in ways that deeply affect our self-esteem, mental health, and overall sense of well-being. Below, we explore some of the most common forms of self-judgment and how they shape our internal experiences.

Guilt and Shame: The Roots of Self-Condemnation

Two of the most powerful emotions tied to self-judgment are guilt and shame. While often used interchangeably, these emotions are quite distinct and operate on different levels.

Guilt is the feeling that arises when we believe we have done something wrong or made a mistake. It is tied to a specific action and is often accompanied by regret.

For example, if you hurt someone's feelings unintentionally, guilt may arise from the belief that you should have acted differently. This self-judgment focuses on behavior—what you did, should have done, or failed to do. While guilt can serve as a catalyst for reflection and positive change, it can also trap you in a cycle of self-blame if not addressed healthily.

Shame, on the other hand, is more insidious. It is the feeling that we are inherently flawed or not good enough. Unlike guilt, which is tied to specific actions, shame is about the self. It convinces us that there is something fundamentally wrong with who we are, making it a deeper and more pervasive form of self-judgment. Shame often manifests in thoughts like "I'm not worthy" or "I don't deserve happiness." It can be debilitating, leading to feelings of isolation, unworthiness, and self-hatred.

Both guilt and shame can keep you trapped in a cycle of self-condemnation, preventing you from forgiving yourself, moving forward, or recognizing your inherent value. They can erode your self-esteem over time, leading to long-term emotional distress if not acknowledged and addressed.

Perfectionism: The Unattainable Standard

Perfectionism is another common manifestation of self-judgment. It is the relentless pursuit of unattainable standards, often rooted in the belief that we must be flawless to be worthy of love, success, or happiness. This form of self-judgment leads to constant self-criticism because perfection is, by nature, impossible to achieve.

Perfectionism creates a mindset where nothing is ever "good enough." Even when we accomplish something significant, we may downplay it, focusing instead on the flaws or areas for improvement. This pattern of thinking leads to a cycle of dissatisfaction, where we constantly strive for an ideal we will never reach.

There are several ways perfectionism shows up in our lives:

Setting unrealistically high standards—We often hold ourselves to standards far higher than we expect from others. Whether in our careers, personal lives, or physical appearance, perfectionism demands excellence in every area. Falling short of these expectations leads to feelings of failure and inadequacy.

Fear of failure—Perfectionists are often paralyzed by the fear of failure. Because they equate their self-worth with their ability to meet their own high standards, they see any mistake or shortcoming as a reflection of their value as a person. This fear can lead to procrastination or avoidance, as we become too afraid to even attempt something if there's a possibility of failure.

Need for validation—Perfectionism often arises from a desire for external validation. We look to others to confirm our worth, and when we don't receive the validation we seek, we feel like we've failed. This can lead to a never-ending cycle of trying to prove ourselves—both to others and ourselves—through accomplishments, appearance, or behavior.

The consequences of perfectionism can be severe. Not only does it lead to chronic stress, but it also fosters a sense of inadequacy that can negatively affect your mental health. You can become trapped in believing that you must always be "better" and that who you are right now is not enough.

Comparison to Others: The Source of Insecurity

Another common form of self-judgment comes from comparing ourselves to others. In a world where social media and societal expectations bombard us with images of success, beauty, and achievement, it is easy to fall into the trap of constantly measuring ourselves against others.

When we compare ourselves, we usually come to one of two conclusions: that we are either superior or inferior to the person we are comparing ourselves to. Both of these judgments are harmful, as they lead to a distorted sense of self-worth.

Feeling inferior—Often, when we compare ourselves to others, we focus on their strengths and successes while ignoring our own. We might see someone who is more successful in their career, has a seemingly perfect relationship, or appears more physically attractive, and we conclude that we are somehow lacking in comparison. This creates feelings of inadequacy, envy, and self-doubt, as we internalize the belief that we are not as valuable or deserving as others.

Feeling superior—On the other hand, sometimes comparison leads to feelings of superiority. We judge others harshly for their perceived shortcomings, thinking, "At least I'm not like them." This form of self-judgment, while seemingly more empowering, is still rooted in insecurity. By comparing ourselves this way, we reinforce that our worth is tied to being "better" than someone else. This keeps us in a competitive mindset, constantly seeking validation through others' failures rather than focusing on personal growth.

External validation—Our tendency to compare ourselves to others is often rooted in a desire for external validation. We look to others to confirm our worth, whether by outperforming them or by aspiring to reach their level of success. However, this external measure of self-worth is fleeting and unreliable, leading to ongoing insecurity. We fail to see our intrinsic value—that we are worthy and whole regardless of how we compare to others.

The comparison trap leads to a negative feedback loop: the more we compare, the more insecure we feel, and the more insecure we feel, the more we compare. It fosters self-doubt, resentment, and a sense of perpetual dissatisfaction, as there will always be someone who appears to have something we don't.

The key to overcoming these patterns of judgment lies in healing the underlying wounds. As we heal our wounds and traumas, the judgment of ourselves begins to dissipate. We learn to accept ourselves as we are, flaws and all. When we embrace self-compassion and love, we no longer need to compare or judge ourselves harshly. In doing so, we create space for growth and transformation.

The Ripple Effect: Healing Judgment of Others

When we heal the judgment we hold against ourselves, something remarkable happens: we stop judging others.

Judgment of others is often a projection of our insecurities and unresolved wounds. We judge others' beliefs, behaviors, and lifestyles because they reflect something within us that we have not yet accepted. Whether it's someone's political stance, religious beliefs, or how they choose to live their life, our judgment of them is ultimately rooted in our inner discord.

Ask yourself:

- In what ways do I judge other people?
- What triggers these judgments?
- Could these judgments be a reflection of something unresolved within me?

When you let go of self-judgment, you no longer need to project your insecurities onto others. What would happen if you took that judgment away? You would begin to see others for who they truly are—unique beings on their soul journey, just as you are. Each person is here to experience life in their own way, and their path is no better or worse than yours. It's simply different.

Accepting others as they are frees you from the burden of judgment. It opens the door to compassion, understanding, and unity.

The Power of Choice in a Polarized Reality

One of the most empowering realizations you can have is that you get to choose how you perceive your reality. You are not a victim of your circumstances; you are the creator of your experiences. In every moment, you can choose how you respond to the situations and people in your life.

When you understand that every experience, no matter how challenging, is an opportunity for growth, you can shift out of the victim mentality and into a place of empowerment. This shift in perception allows you to see your life from a higher perspective, recognizing that all experiences have value.

Fear is one of the primary emotions that keeps us stuck in polarity. Fear of the unknown, fear of those who are different from us, and fear of failure all stem from the belief that we are separate and powerless. But when we release fear and embrace love, we transcend the limitations of polarity and step into our highest potential.

Moving Beyond Polarity: Choosing Your Timeline

As you ascend into higher frequencies, you can move beyond polarity and create a reality based on love, unity, and harmony. Multiple timelines exist for Earth right now, each reflecting different levels of consciousness. You have the power to choose which timeline you want to experience.

What you focus on expands. If you focus on fear, conflict, and division, you will remain in a polarized reality where those experiences dominate. But if you focus on love, compassion, and unity, you will align yourself with the higher dimensional timeline where peace and harmony prevail.

To fully step into this higher timeline, you must be willing to let go of the old stories, beliefs, and judgments that no longer serve you. This includes turning off the news, releasing the need to engage in political drama, and focusing on your inner growth. When you focus on healing yourself, you naturally shift into a higher vibration and align with a timeline that reflects that energy.

Transmuting Fear and Judgment Into Love

The process of transmuting fear and judgment into love is essential for our personal and collective ascension. There are many ways to do this, whether through meditation, energy work, or inner reflection. The goal is to release the lower vibrational emotions that keep us trapped in polarity and open ourselves to the higher frequencies of love, compassion, and acceptance.

One of the most powerful ways to transmute fear is to face your inner demons head-on. This requires courage and vulnerability, but through this process, you can heal the wounds that keep you in fear. As you release your inner trauma and judgment, you will naturally raise your vibration.

Acceptance is the antidote to judgment. When you can accept yourself and others without the need to label, change, or control, you free yourself from the polarity of good and bad. This practice allows you to rise above duality and live from a place of unconditional love.

By understanding polarity from a higher perspective, you can release the fear and judgment that hold you back, allowing you to choose a higher vibrational timeline. Moving beyond polarity and embracing love, compassion, and unity opens the door to your highest potential and spiritual ascension.

In the next chapter, we will focus on applying these principles in your everyday life—in your relationships, work, and interactions with the world around you.

CHAPTER 4

EMBODYING UNITY AND NON-JUDGMENT IN YOUR RELATIONSHIPS, WORK, AND DAILY LIFE

In the previous chapter, we explored the concept of polarity and how judgment arises from living in a world of contrasts. By moving beyond judgment and embracing neutrality and acceptance, you can live in greater harmony with yourself and others.

By embodying these principles in all areas of your life, you not only maintain alignment with your highest self, but you also contribute to creating a more compassionate, unified, and peaceful environment for yourself and those around you.

Embodying Non-Judgment in Relationships

Relationships are among the most important areas where polarity and judgment often arise. Whether with family, friends, colleagues, or romantic partners, your interactions with others can easily trigger judgments, comparisons, and feelings of separation. But by embracing non-judgment and practicing compassionate neutrality, you can transform your relationships into spaces of harmony, growth, and mutual respect.

Deep listening is one of the most powerful ways to embody non-judgment in relationships. When someone shares their thoughts or feelings, practice listening without immediately forming judgments or assumptions. Simply be present and hold space for their experience. This strengthens your connection and creates a safe environment for open and honest communication.

Often, judgment arises when others don't meet our expectations of how they should behave, think, or act. To embody non-judgment, practice releasing these expectations and allowing others to be who they are without needing them to conform to your ideals. By accepting others as they are, you foster more authentic and harmonious relationships.

As you interact with others, remind yourself that every person you encounter reflects yourself. Their actions, beliefs, and experiences are expressions of their path, just as yours are expressions of your journey. Recognizing this makes releasing judgment and approaching others with empathy and understanding easier.

Bringing Compassion and Acceptance Into the Workplace

The workplace is often a space where polarity and judgment are magnified. Whether dealing with competition, office politics, or differing perspectives, work environments can be breeding grounds for separation and comparison. However, by embodying the principles of unity, non-judgment, and acceptance, you can create a more harmonious and productive work experience—for yourself and those around you.

In collaborative work environments, differing opinions and approaches are inevitable. Instead of judging others' ideas or methods as right or wrong, practice embracing diversity of thought. Recognize that each person brings their unique strengths and perspectives to the table. By valuing this diversity, you create a more innovative and inclusive work environment.

Judgment often arises in the workplace when we compare ourselves to others—whether in terms of performance, recognition, or success. To embody non-judgment, practice releasing the need to compete or compare. Focus instead on your growth, contribution, and alignment with your purpose. When you let go of comparison, you free yourself from the stress of trying to measure up to others and create space for greater fulfillment in your work.

Leading with compassion and acceptance can inspire those around you to do the same. Offer support to your colleagues, recognize their contributions, and create an atmosphere where everyone feels valued. When you embody non-judgment in the workplace, you not only enhance your own experience but also elevate the team's collective energy.

Navigating Interactions With the World From a Place of Unity

The world is filled with contrasts—differing opinions, cultural perspectives, and societal challenges. It's easy to judge others, especially when faced with viewpoints or behaviors that don't align with our own. But by embracing unity and recognizing our interconnectedness, we can navigate the world with more compassion, openness, and acceptance.

Many judgments come from a desire to prove that we are "right" and others are "wrong." This creates division and reinforces the illusion of separation. To embody unity, practice letting go of the need to be right. Instead of focusing on differences, seek to understand the deeper truth that connects all perspectives. By approaching others with curiosity and a willingness to learn, you open yourself to new insights and foster greater harmony.

Unity consciousness reminds us that all beings are interconnected. Every person, animal, and living creature is a part of the same web of life, and each is here to play a unique role in the evolution of consciousness.

When you embody this understanding, it becomes easier to extend compassion to all—regardless of their background, beliefs, or actions. Practicing compassion toward others, even those who may seem different or difficult to understand, helps dissolve the illusion of separation and brings more unity into the world.

We face challenges such as social injustice, political divisions, and environmental crises. Instead of judging these situations as "bad" or "hopeless," practice reframing them as opportunities for growth and collective evolution. Ask yourself: How can I contribute to the solution? What role can I play in bringing about positive change? By shifting your perspective from judgment to active participation, you align with timelines where solutions and healing become possible.

Maintaining Alignment With Your Highest Self

As you embody the principles of unity, non-judgment, and acceptance in your relationships, work, and interactions with the world, it's essential to maintain alignment with your highest self. Your highest self is the aspect of you that connects to unconditional love, wisdom, and purpose. When you stay aligned with this version of yourself, you can navigate life's challenges with grace, integrity, and clarity.

To maintain alignment with your highest self, incorporate daily practices that support your connection to this aspect of yourself. This might include meditation, journaling, or setting intentions for how you want to show up in the world. Regularly tuning into your higher self helps you stay grounded in love, compassion, and higher wisdom, even when external circumstances are challenging.

Every day, you are presented with choices—how to respond to a situation, treat others, or approach your goals. Before making decisions, take a moment to check in with your highest self. Ask yourself: Does this choice align with my highest self? Does it reflect love, unity, and integrity? By making choices from a place of alignment, you ensure that your actions are in harmony with your greater purpose and contribute to creating positive timelines.

Your intuition is the voice of your higher self guiding you in each moment. To maintain alignment, practice listening to and trusting your inner guidance. When faced with uncertainty or difficult situations, tune into your intuition and allow it to guide you toward the actions that are in your highest good. By following this inner wisdom, you stay aligned with the path that leads to your greatest growth and fulfillment.

Creating Ripple Effects of Unity and Compassion

When you embody the principles of non-judgment, unity, and compassion in your life, you naturally create ripple effects that extend to those around you. Your energy, actions, and words can influence others positively, helping them shift out of judgment and into greater awareness and compassion.

Leading by example is one of the most powerful ways to inspire change. When you embody unity, non-judgment, and acceptance in your relationships, work, and interactions, others will naturally take notice. Your calm, grounded energy will inspire those around you to reflect on their own judgments and shift toward more compassionate ways of being.

As you navigate your relationships and interactions, practice holding space for others to grow at their own pace. Not everyone is ready to release judgment or embrace unity, and that's okay. By offering patience, understanding, and support, you create an environment where others feel safe to explore their growth journey without fear of judgment.

Each time you choose to embody non-judgment and compassion, you contribute to the collective energy of unity on Earth. The more individuals align with this way of being, the more the collective consciousness shifts toward love, harmony, and connection. Your personal transformation has a powerful ripple effect, helping to create a world where unity, peace, and compassion are the norm.

By practicing deep listening, releasing expectations, and fostering compassion, you can create more harmonious and authentic connections with others. In the workplace, embodying these principles leads to greater collaboration, support, and fulfillment. In your interactions with the world, you can help dissolve the illusion of separation by embracing diversity and extending compassion to all beings.

By staying aligned with your highest self, you maintain a strong foundation of love, wisdom, and integrity, allowing you to navigate challenges gracefully and clearly.

The next chapter will explore the importance of self-healing and embracing compassion.

CHAPTER 5

HEALING SELF-JUDGMENT AND EMBRACING COMPASSION

Much of the judgment we project onto others stems from our unresolved wounds. Whether it's feelings of guilt, shame, or inadequacy, these emotions often reflect our internal struggle with self-judgment. In a polarized world, we measure ourselves against external standards, and this comparison leads to feelings of inferiority or superiority as we seek to validate our worth. To truly move beyond the judgment of others, we must first look inward and heal the judgment we place on ourselves.

Self-judgment can take many forms—guilt, perfectionism, comparison to others—but at its core, it arises from the belief that we are not enough as we are. This chapter will explore how to recognize, heal, and ultimately release self-judgment, allowing you to cultivate self-compassion and love. When you embrace yourself fully, flaws and all, you will be free from the cycle of judgment and create space for growth and transformation.

Recognizing Self-Judgment: The Roots of Guilt, Shame, and Comparison

Self-judgment often manifests subtly, but its effects can be deeply felt. It shows up as guilt, shame, perfectionism, and the constant need to compare ourselves to others. These forms of self-judgment are rooted in the conditioning we've received from society, family, and the collective consciousness, which teaches us that we must earn our worth by meeting external standards.

As I mentioned in an earlier chapter, guilt arises when we believe we've done something wrong or failed to meet our own or others' expectations. It leads to feelings of unworthiness and self-blame. Shame, on the other hand, is a deeper form of self-judgment—it makes us feel as though we are inherently flawed or defective. Both emotions keep us trapped in a cycle of self-condemnation and prevent us from seeing our true worth.

Many of us hold ourselves to impossible standards, constantly striving to be "better" or to meet societal expectations of success, beauty, or intelligence. Perfectionism is a form of self-judgment that causes you to feel inadequate when you inevitably fall short of these unrealistic goals. It fuels feelings of failure, disappointment, and exhaustion as you chase an ever-moving target.

When we compare ourselves to others, we either judge ourselves as inferior or superior. This comparison is rooted in the belief that we must compete with others to prove our worth, and it perpetuates feelings of separation and inadequacy. Whether we feel we are "better" or "worse" than someone else, comparison disconnects us from our inherent value and uniqueness.

The Impact of Self-Judgment on Your Life

Self-judgment affects every aspect of your life—your relationships, work, health, and self-esteem. It creates a constant sense of pressure and self-criticism that can be overwhelming and debilitating. When you judge yourself, you are more likely to project that judgment onto others, reinforcing feelings of separation and conflict.

The constant inner dialogue of self-criticism drains your emotional energy. Living under the weight of self-judgment leaves little room for joy, creativity, or fulfillment. This emotional exhaustion can lead to stress, anxiety, and burnout as you are constantly striving to "prove" yourself or avoid feelings of inadequacy.

Self-judgment can often spill over into your relationships. When you judge yourself harshly, you are more likely to judge others or seek validation from them to compensate for your feelings of inadequacy. This creates a dynamic of comparison and criticism, which can strain relationships and prevent authentic connection.

Self-judgment keeps you locked in a cycle of self-doubt and fear of failure. When you believe you are not enough, you are less likely to take risks, pursue your dreams, or embrace new opportunities. The fear of judgment and failure becomes a barrier to growth and expansion, limiting your ability to step into your full potential.

Healing Self-Judgment: The Path to Self-Compassion

The key to overcoming patterns of self-judgment lies in healing the underlying wounds. These wounds may be rooted in childhood experiences, societal conditioning, or past traumas, but they can be healed with compassion, awareness, and self-acceptance. As you heal these wounds, the judgment of yourself begins to dissipate, and you learn to embrace yourself fully—flaws and all.

The first step to healing self-judgment is acknowledging the wounds that drive it. Reflect on where your guilt, shame, or inadequacy comes from. Are they rooted in specific experiences or beliefs? By bringing awareness to these wounds, you create space for healing and transformation. Journaling or meditative reflection can be powerful tools for uncovering these underlying emotions.

Self-compassion is the antidote to self-judgment. It involves treating yourself with the same kindness, care, and understanding you would offer a friend. When you make a mistake or fall short of your expectations, instead of criticizing yourself, practice self-forgiveness and acceptance. Remind yourself that you are human and imperfection is part of the journey. Self-compassion helps break the cycle of judgment and opens the door to healing.

To heal self-judgment, you must also release the need for perfectionism. Understand that striving for perfection is a form of self-judgment that traps you in a cycle of inadequacy. Accept that you are enough just as you are, and that growth is a process, not a destination. Give yourself permission to make mistakes and embrace the lessons they bring.

Shifting from Comparison to Self-Acceptance

Comparison is a major source of self-judgment based on the illusion that you must compete with others to prove your worth. The truth is that each of us is on our own unique journey, and there is no need to compare ourselves to anyone else. Shifting from comparison to self-acceptance allows you to celebrate your path without needing to measure yourself against external standards.

Instead of comparing yourself to others, focus on your unique qualities and strengths. What makes you special? What gifts do you bring to the world? By embracing your uniqueness, you stop trying to fit into a mold created by others and begin to live authentically. Celebrate your individuality, knowing your path is just as valid and valuable as anyone else's.

Often, we compare ourselves to others because we seek external validation. We want to know we are "enough" by society's standards. But true self-worth comes from within, not from the approval of others. Practice affirming your value and worthiness, independent of how you compare to others. This shift from external validation to self-acceptance helps you let go of judgment and embrace your inherent value.

When you release comparison, you free yourself to celebrate the success and uniqueness of others without feeling diminished. Recognize that someone else's achievements or qualities do not detract from your own. There is enough success, love, and abundance to go around. By celebrating others, you shift from a mindset of lack to one of abundance, fostering deeper connection and joy.

Embracing Self-Love and Acceptance for Transformation

The ultimate goal of healing self-judgment is to embrace self-love and acceptance. When you love yourself fully, you no longer need to compare, judge, or criticize yourself. You see yourself as worthy of love, compassion, and growth, just as you are. This self-acceptance creates space for transformation and allows you to step into your true power.

Self-love is a practice, not a destination. Incorporate daily rituals of self-care and self-affirmation into your life. Whether it's through meditation, positive affirmations, or simply taking time for yourself, these practices help reinforce your belief in your worthiness. The more you nurture your relationship with yourself, the easier it becomes to release judgment and embrace love.

Use positive affirmations to reinforce self-love and acceptance. Affirmations such as "I am enough just as I am," "I deserve love and compassion," or "I embrace my imperfections as part of my journey" can help shift your mindset from self-judgment to self-acceptance. Repeating these affirmations daily helps reprogram your subconscious mind and reinforces your sense of worthiness.

Self-acceptance doesn't mean complacency—it means acknowledging where you are while allowing yourself to grow and evolve. Embrace your growth journey without judgment, knowing that every experience, success, and failure is part of your evolution. Accepting yourself as you are creates the foundation for meaningful transformation.

The Ripple Effect of Healing Self-Judgment

As you heal self-judgment and embrace self-compassion, you naturally extend that compassion to others. When you are no longer harshly judging yourself, you are less likely to judge others. This shift in your inner world creates a ripple effect in your relationships, work, and interactions with the world.

As you heal your wounds and release self-judgment, you project love and acceptance onto others. You see them through the lens of compassion rather than judgment, understanding that everyone is on their journey. This shift creates more harmonious and authentic relationships, fostering deeper connections with those around you.

When you stop judging yourself, you also stop holding others to impossible standards. You create space for them to grow and evolve. This allows for more supportive and nurturing relationships where both you and others feel free to be your authentic selves.

As you heal your self-judgment, you contribute to the collective healing of humanity. The more individuals who release self-criticism and embrace self-compassion, the more we shift the collective consciousness toward love, unity, and acceptance. By healing yourself, you play a powerful role in creating a more compassionate and harmonious world.

By embracing your unique path, releasing the need for comparison, and practicing daily self-love, you can cultivate a sense of inner peace and fulfillment. This healing not only transforms your relationship with yourself but also creates a ripple effect of love and compassion in your relationships and the world.

The Connection Between Healing and Spiritual Evolution

Your spiritual evolution is intimately connected to the process of self-healing. When you heal self-judgment, you create space for higher awareness, a deeper connection with your soul, and a greater ability to receive guidance from your higher self. This healing process allows you to shed the layers of conditioning holding you back, revealing your true spiritual essence.

Self-heal as a gateway to spiritual awakening—Healing your inner wounds—whether they are based on guilt, shame, or unworthiness—enables you to step into a higher state of consciousness. Each time you release a self-limiting belief or judgment, you clear space for your higher self to shine through. This process of letting go of old patterns is a key part of spiritual evolution, as it brings you closer to your true nature.

Higher self as your guide to fulfillment—As you heal and release self-judgment, you strengthen your connection to your higher self. Your higher self is the version of you that exists beyond fear, doubt, and ego; it operates from a place of love, wisdom, and divine purpose. The more you align with this aspect of yourself, the easier it becomes to access the guidance and clarity you need to fulfill your soul's mission.

Clear energetic blocks—Self-judgment creates energetic blocks that prevent you from accessing higher frequencies of consciousness. These blocks can keep you stuck in lower vibrational timelines where you feel limited or disconnected from your purpose. By healing self-judgment, you dissolve these blocks and raise your vibration, allowing you to step into higher timelines where your spiritual growth and soul's purpose can flourish.

How Healing Self-Judgment Enhances Manifestation

One of the most significant ways healing self-judgment impacts your life is by enhancing your ability to manifest. Manifestation brings your desires into reality by aligning your thoughts, emotions, and energy. When self-judgment is present, it creates resistance that can block the manifestation process. By healing these internal barriers, you free yourself to create and attract the life you truly desire.

Releasing Resistance to Manifestation

Self-judgment is one of the most significant sources of resistance when manifesting your desires. This resistance often takes the form of limiting beliefs—the internal stories you tell yourself about why you're not deserving or capable of receiving what you want.

For example, thoughts like *I'm not worthy of success* or *I don't deserve love* act as energetic barriers preventing the flow of abundance, love, and fulfillment into your life. These beliefs block the manifestation process because they send conflicting signals to the universe, even when you are consciously trying to create positive change.

When you carry self-judgment and limiting beliefs, it's as though you're trying to move forward with the brakes on. No matter how hard you push or how clear your intentions are, the resistance caused by these internal barriers keeps you stuck in place, unable to fully receive the blessings you seek. The universe is always responding to the energy you project, and if part of you believes you are unworthy or incapable, that energy will be reflected back to you in the form of blocked manifestations.

Healing and replacing these judgments with self-acceptance is key to releasing the resistance holding you back. When you recognize your inherent worth and let go of the belief that you are not enough, you dismantle the walls preventing you from receiving. This doesn't happen overnight, but as you consciously work on releasing self-judgment, you'll notice that your manifestations come more easily and in greater alignment with your desires.

Manifesting from a Place of Alignment

When you free yourself from self-judgment and limiting beliefs, you step into a state of alignment with your true self. This is the place where authentic and powerful manifestation occurs. Instead of trying to manifest from a place of lack, fear, or insecurity, you create from a place of wholeness and self-worth.

Manifesting from lack often looks like trying to fill a void or proving something to yourself or others. It's driven by the fear that you are not enough as you are, and so you need external achievements, relationships, or possessions to feel validated. However, when you are still entangled in self-judgment, these manifestations—if they arrive at all—often don't bring lasting fulfillment. The underlying belief of not being good enough continues to color the experience, no matter what you accomplish or attract.

In contrast, manifesting from a place of alignment means creating from a sense of self-love, empowerment, and inner completeness. When you no longer judge yourself harshly or feel the need to prove your worth, the things you manifest come from a higher vibration. You attract experiences, opportunities, and relationships that resonate with your authentic self rather than things rooted in fear or ego-driven desires.

This shift in energy allows your manifestations to flow more easily and with greater clarity. When you align with your soul's purpose and are free from self-criticism, you naturally attract experiences that support your highest good. You are no longer chasing after things to compensate for perceived shortcomings.

Instead, you create from a place of expansion, joy, and possibility. This makes the manifestation process smoother and accelerates your ability to step into your highest timeline—the version of reality that aligns with your deepest desires and fullest potential.

Expanding Your Capacity to Receive

Another profound effect of healing self-judgment is that it expands your capacity to receive. Often, feelings of unworthiness or guilt cause us to subconsciously push away the very things we want to manifest—whether that's love, success, or abundance. This happens because, deep down, we don't believe we are worthy of receiving these things, or we feel guilty for wanting more.

For example, someone who believes they don't deserve love might sabotage relationships, or someone who feels unworthy of success may procrastinate or settle for less than they are capable of. These subconscious patterns create a self-fulfilling prophecy where the lack of worthiness leads to missed opportunities and unfulfilled desires, reinforcing the original belief.

Healing these feelings of unworthiness through self-compassion and self-acceptance opens the door to greater abundance. When you fully accept and love yourself, you naturally begin to see yourself as deserving of the love, success, and prosperity you seek. You shift your mindset from one of scarcity and limitation to one of openness and possibility. Expanding your capacity to receive makes it easier for the universe to deliver the blessings you desire because there is no longer any internal resistance blocking the flow.

Self-compassion and acceptance also teach you that there is no need to feel guilty for wanting more in life. You realize that the universe is infinitely abundant, and by embracing your worthiness to receive, you are not taking away from anyone else. There is more than enough for everyone, and your ability to receive is directly tied to your belief that you are worthy of those gifts.

When you heal self-judgment and expand your capacity to receive, you increase your manifestation power. You become a magnet for what you desire because your energy aligns with receiving rather than resisting. You trust that you are worthy of all the good the universe has to offer, strengthening your ability to manifest effortlessly.

The Power of Self-Acceptance in Manifestation

Releasing self-judgment is a critical step in removing the resistance that blocks manifestation. Limiting beliefs such as *I'm not good enough* or *I don't deserve success* create energetic barriers that prevent you from fully receiving the abundance, love, and fulfillment the universe is ready to offer. By healing these judgments and cultivating self-acceptance, you dissolve the resistance holding you back, allowing your desires to flow more easily into your life.

Manifesting from a place of alignment with your true self amplifies your creative power. When you are no longer driven by fear or lack but by wholeness and authenticity, you attract opportunities and experiences that resonate with your soul's purpose. This shift in energy accelerates your manifestations and aligns you with your highest timeline, where you are living your most empowered and fulfilled life.

Finally, healing self-judgment expands your capacity to receive. By embracing self-compassion and releasing feelings of unworthiness or guilt, you open yourself to the infinite possibilities that the universe offers. You see yourself as deserving of all the good in life, which strengthens your ability to manifest with ease.

Through self-acceptance and alignment, you become a powerful creator of your reality, capable of manifesting from a place of abundance, wholeness, and authenticity.

By releasing limiting beliefs, embracing self-compassion, and aligning with your higher self, you open yourself to greater clarity, abundance, and fulfillment. As you step into this new reality, you manifest a life that reflects your highest potential, bringing your deepest desires and soul's mission into alignment.

In the next chapter, we will explore how recognizing yourself as a multidimensional being can help you release judgment and embrace the diversity of human experiences.

CHAPTER 6

EMBRACING THE DIVERSITY
OF SOUL JOURNEYS AND
RELEASING CONTROL

We are all here on Earth to have unique experiences that express our soul's journey. These diverse experiences contribute to the evolution and expansion of Source energy itself. Every person's life is a chapter in their individual soul story, and collectively, our experiences are constantly being fed back to Source, allowing for the expansion and evolution of the universe.

When we accept that each person's path is valid and necessary for their evolution, we no longer feel the need to control or change others. Instead, we recognize that every soul is on its own journey, and we can allow space for greater compassion, understanding, and acceptance.

We Are Multidimensional Beings with Countless Lifetimes

One of the key principles of spiritual evolution is the understanding that we are multidimensional beings. The singular life we are living now is just one expression of our soul's infinite journey. Over countless lifetimes, we have played different roles, experienced various challenges, and learned through the spectrum of polarity—the contrasts of good and bad, right and wrong, light and dark.

In this multidimensional journey, we have experienced both sides of the coin. We have been the hero and the villain, the oppressor and the oppressed, the seeker of truth, and the one who hides from it. We have chosen all of these roles before incarnating, knowing that each one offers valuable lessons and opportunities for growth. Understanding makes it easier to release judgment of ourselves and others.

Every experience we encounter—whether joyful or painful, easy or challenging—serves a purpose in our soul's evolution. Each lifetime adds to the depth and richness of our understanding, expanding our consciousness and contributing to the collective growth of humanity and Source. When we view our lives through the lens of soul evolution, we can see that every experience is meaningful, and every role is necessary.

Before each incarnation, we enter into soul contracts—agreements made on a higher level about the experiences we will have, the people we will meet, and the lessons we will learn. These contracts are not random; they are carefully chosen to help us grow and evolve as souls. By acknowledging that we, too, have played every role and made every choice, we can release the need to judge others for their current life circumstances.

The Amusement Park of Earth: Exploring the Infinite Rides of the Soul's Journey

Imagine Earth as the most intricate and expansive amusement park ever conceived, where every country, culture, and human experience represents a different ride or attraction that a soul can choose to experience. In this vast park, there are no wrong choices, no inherently "good" or "bad" experiences—just a diverse array of opportunities for growth, learning, and adventure.

Before incarnating, each soul stands at the entrance to this cosmic amusement park, eagerly surveying the landscape of possibilities. In this park, every country is a unique ride—each with its own distinct flavor, set of challenges, and rewards. Just as visitors to a theme park select different rides based on what excites or intrigues them, souls also choose specific incarnations based on what they want to explore, experience, and evolve through.

The Variety of Experiences

Some souls may choose to experience life in a country steeped in ancient traditions, where the focus might be on spiritual exploration or deep cultural heritage. Others may be drawn to countries experiencing rapid technological advancement and modernity, where the lessons revolve around innovation, progress, and adapting to a fast-changing world.

Rides of Wealth and Poverty—Some souls may choose to incarnate into lives of great material wealth, where the challenges revolve around responsibility, the use of power, and how to find meaning beyond possessions. Others might choose experiences of poverty, where the lessons are about resilience, resourcefulness, and understanding that true wealth lies within. Neither experience is superior; they are just different pathways of learning.

Rides of Health and Illness—In this amusement park, some souls might opt for incarnations to experience vibrant health, with lessons centered on vitality, physical expression, and embodiment. Others may choose to experience illness or disability, where the deeper lessons involve patience, compassion, and discovering inner strength despite physical limitations. The diversity of these experiences helps the soul understand the full range of human potential, from strength to vulnerability.

Rides of Conflict and Peace—Certain souls may choose to incarnate in regions experiencing conflict, whether political, social, or even within families. These souls may seek to understand human dynamics through the lens of war, struggle, or division. The lessons here might involve courage, advocacy, or learning the consequences of aggression. Conversely, some souls choose peaceful environments to focus on creativity, cooperation, and harmony. Again, neither is "good" or "bad." Each ride is simply a different way to explore human nature and consciousness.

No Good or Bad, Only Experience

Just as there's no "right" way to visit an amusement park, there is no right way to live a human life. Some might choose a leisurely ride on the Ferris wheel, enjoying the slow, panoramic view of life, while others might dive headfirst into the thrill of a roller coaster, filled with twists, turns, and moments of intense exhilaration.

A soul's choice to incarnate into a life of privilege doesn't make it more fortunate than the soul who chooses hardship. It's akin to choosing different levels of intensity in the amusement park. Some rides are calm and gentle, while others are wild and unpredictable. Both have value, teach unique lessons, and are necessary for the park to offer a full range of experiences.

From the soul's perspective, the goal is not to avoid challenges but to engage with them. Just as a visitor to an amusement park wouldn't consider a thrilling ride "bad" simply because it's intense, a soul doesn't see suffering, hardship, or adversity as inherently negative. These experiences are valuable for the growth they offer.

The Soul's Perspective

From the soul's perspective, the Earth amusement park is a place where they can experience duality, growth, and the full spectrum of emotions. A soul doesn't judge its incarnation based on societal values of success, failure, or material gain. Instead, it views each life as a chapter in a much longer journey of self-discovery and expansion.

Some souls may incarnate in periods of war, where they experience intense emotions like fear, anger, and the struggle for survival. Others might choose peaceful times, where the lessons are about nurturing, growth, and the pursuit of creative expression. In the amusement park of Earth, these varied experiences are seen as equally valuable opportunities for the soul to evolve.

Multiple Lives, Multiple Rides

Just as an amusement park visitor might ride multiple attractions during their visit, the soul reincarnates and experiences different lifetimes to explore a wide range of human experiences. Over many lifetimes, a soul might experience life in different countries, social classes, and genders, taking on various roles—teacher, warrior, healer, artist, and so on. Through these multiple incarnations, the soul accumulates wisdom and a broader perspective on what it means to be human.

- A soul might choose a life as a male in one lifetime and a female in another, learning the unique strengths, perspectives, and lessons each experience offers.
- A soul might experience life as a political leader in one lifetime and as a revolutionary in another, learning the dynamics of power and resistance from both sides.

Each ride provides a unique viewpoint, a chance for the soul to see a different facet of the human experience. These varied experiences contribute to expanding the soul's understanding of the world and its place within it.

The Playground of Duality

As an amusement park, Earth is also the ultimate playground of duality. It offers rides in both light and dark, allowing souls to explore opposites such as love and fear, success and failure, peace and conflict, joy and sorrow. This duality provides the contrast necessary for growth. Just as light becomes more meaningful after experiencing darkness, souls grow through encountering both ends of the spectrum in their incarnations.

This playground of duality isn't meant to be a punishment or a test—it's an opportunity. From the soul's higher perspective, the challenges of life are seen as stepping stones to greater understanding, not something to be avoided or feared. Whether the soul rides the smooth carousel or the tumultuous roller coaster, it does so with the understanding that both are part of the same park—both serve a purpose in its journey of expansion.

Enjoying the Ride

In the grand amusement park of Earth, souls come to experience the richness of life in all its forms. There is no good or bad, only a spectrum of opportunities for growth and exploration. Just as in any amusement park, the thrill comes not from sticking to the easiest rides but from embracing the full range of experiences, whether they be joyful or challenging.

The soul understands that each life is a temporary ride, a single adventure in a much longer journey. With each incarnation, the soul learns more about itself, others, and the nature of existence. And when it's ready, the soul steps off the ride, only to choose another, knowing there is always more to learn and experience in this vast cosmic amusement park.

Releasing Judgment by Seeing the Bigger Picture

When we recognize that we have lived countless lifetimes and that each person's current life is just one chapter in their larger soul story, we can release the need to judge or control others. Instead of seeing someone's behavior or choices as "good" or "bad," we begin to see the bigger picture—that their experiences serve a purpose in their evolution, just as ours are in ours.

Judgment often arises from the belief that some actions are inherently "good" while others are inherently "bad." But when viewed from the perspective of soul growth, these labels lose their meaning. Every experience—whether we perceive it as positive or negative—offers opportunities for learning and transformation. What may seem "bad" in one lifetime may provide the catalyst for a soul's greatest growth. By letting go of rigid judgments, we free ourselves from the limitations of dualistic thinking.

Each person's life is designed to teach them specific soul lessons. These lessons may not always be apparent to others and may come in the form of challenges, hardships, or difficult relationships. By recognizing that every individual is working through their own lessons, we can approach them with greater compassion and understanding. Instead of trying to change or fix them, we can hold space for their growth and trust that they are exactly where they need to be on their journey.

When we judge others, it often comes from a desire to control or change them. We believe if they just thought or acted differently, they would be better off. But this desire to control is rooted in the illusion that we know what is best for someone else's soul journey. The truth is, we cannot know the intricacies of another person's path. By releasing the need to control, we allow others the freedom to experience life in their own way, trusting that their soul knows what it needs for growth and evolution.

What Happens When We Accept Others as They Are?

Accepting others for who and what they are creates a space of non-judgment and unconditional love. This acceptance allows us to move beyond the need to critique, compare, or control, and instead, we begin to see the beauty in each person's unique journey.

When we stop trying to control others, we free ourselves from the burden of constantly evaluating their choices. We recognize that each soul is on its journey, and their experiences—though different from ours—are valid and necessary. This creates a sense of inner peace, as we no longer need to impose our beliefs or expectations on others. We simply allow them to be who they are, trusting in the wisdom of their path.

Acceptance fosters greater compassion for others. When we understand that every person is living out their soul's lessons, we become more empathetic toward their struggles, challenges, and choices. We no longer judge them based on superficial criteria; instead, we honor the depth of their journey. Compassion helps us build deeper, more authentic connections with others, rooted in love and understanding rather than judgment.

Embracing the diversity of human experiences brings us closer to a sense of unity. Rather than seeing differences as something to fear or judge, we begin to celebrate them as part of the richness of life. Each soul's journey adds to the collective tapestry of humanity, and by accepting this diversity, we contribute to a more harmonious and unified world. When we release judgment and embrace acceptance, we move from separation to unity, recognizing that we are all interconnected.

The Freedom of Allowing Others to Grow

Allowing others to grow and evolve on their own terms is one of the greatest gifts we can give them—and ourselves. When we let go of judgment and the need to control, we create a space where others can flourish and release themselves from the emotional burden of trying to direct someone else's path.

Each soul grows at its own pace, and every individual is at a different point in their evolutionary journey. By allowing others the freedom to grow without interference, we honor their process. This doesn't mean we agree with or condone every action; rather, we trust that their soul knows what it needs to experience for its evolution. We hold space for their growth without judgment or expectation.

Often, our desire to control others stems from an attachment to specific outcomes. We want others to behave in a way that makes us feel more comfortable or aligns with our beliefs. But by releasing this attachment, we free ourselves from the disappointment or frustration that comes when people don't meet our expectations. Letting go allows us to live with more ease and flow, trusting that everything is unfolding as it should.

When we stop trying to change others, we create a space for their authentic transformation. People are more likely to grow and evolve when they feel accepted rather than judged or pressured to change. By offering unconditional love and support, we contribute to an environment where transformation can occur naturally, without force or manipulation.

Living in Harmony with Yourself and Others

When we accept that everyone is on their unique soul journey, we begin to live in greater harmony with ourselves and others. This harmony is born from the understanding that each experience—both ours and others—is part of a larger plan for soul evolution. By releasing judgment and control, we create a life filled with peace, compassion, and unity.

Acceptance brings a profound sense of inner peace. When we no longer feel the need to control or judge others, we free up mental and emotional energy we can direct toward our growth and fulfillment. This peace allows us to move through life with more grace, knowing that we align with the flow of the universe.

Compassion becomes a natural way of being when we release judgment. We see others not as competitors or threats, but as fellow souls on the journey of life. Compassion helps us build deeper connections, foster understanding, and create a more loving and supportive environment for ourselves and others.

By embracing the diversity of human experiences and releasing judgment, we contribute to creating a world based on unity rather than division. Each of us plays a role in this collective evolution, and by living in alignment with these principles, we help elevate the consciousness of humanity as a whole. Together, we co-create a reality based on acceptance, love, and the shared recognition of our interconnectedness.

By recognizing that every person is on their unique soul journey, we can release the need to judge or control others. Accepting others as they are allows us to live in greater harmony, fostering compassion, understanding, and unity.

When we stop trying to change or critique others, we free ourselves from the emotional burden of judgment and open the door to deeper, more meaningful connections. This acceptance creates a world where each person is honored for their individuality, and where we collectively contribute to the evolution of Source through our diverse experiences.

In the next chapter, we will explore the nature of your energetic self, how your vibrational frequency shapes your reality, and how raising that vibration can unlock deeper experiences and connections.

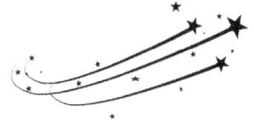

CHAPTER 7

HARNESSING YOUR ENERGETIC POWER: UNLOCKING THE FLOW OF HIGHER VIBRATIONS

Everything in the universe, including us, is made up of energy. On the surface, we appear as solid, physical beings. But beneath that physical form, we are far more energy than matter. The realization that you are energy has profound implications for how you experience reality, how you evolve, and how you can influence the course of your life. Your energetic frequency not only creates your experience of reality but also determines how you interact with the world around you, from your personal relationships to the broader, unseen dimensions of existence.

In this chapter, we will explore the essence of your energetic self, the ways in which your vibrational frequency shapes your reality, and how elevating that frequency can open the door to richer experiences and connections. We will also touch on the importance of calming your nervous system, the changes happening in your body to hold more energy, and the latent potential within your DNA that becomes activated as your energy rises.

The Energy Behind Reality

You are more than just your body, thoughts, or emotions. At your core, you are a being of energy, vibrating at a particular frequency. This energy field interacts with everything around you, creating your experience of reality. Everything in your life is influenced by the energy you emit.

Think of yourself as a radio transmitter, constantly broadcasting your unique, energetic signature out into the world. This signature, or vibration, determines the experiences and relationships you attract into your life. Like attracts like in the energetic realm, so whatever frequency you are vibrating at, you will attract more of the same.

Low-Vibration Experiences: The Cycle of Fear, Anger, and Frustration

When you are feeling fear, anger, or frustration, you are operating at a lower frequency. These low-vibrational states create an energetic field that resonates with similar frequencies in your environment, which means that, energetically, you begin to attract experiences that match this lower vibration. This might include more stress, conflict, or challenges in your life, whether in your relationships, career, or personal well-being.

For example, when you're feeling frustrated or angry, you may notice that things tend to go wrong more frequently. Traffic delays, misunderstandings with others, or unexpected obstacles seem to pop up, reinforcing the negative emotions you're already experiencing. This isn't just a coincidence; it reflects the energy you are emitting and the law of attraction at work. Your lower vibrational state attracts similar energy, creating a cycle where negativity begets more negativity.

Similarly, fear tends to attract situations that confirm the fears you hold. If you're operating from a place of fear—fear of failure, fear of rejection, or fear of the unknown—you'll find that opportunities slip away, challenges multiply, and relationships become strained. Fear clouds your ability to see possibilities and blocks your intuition, keeping you locked in a state where stress and struggle become the norm.

Low-vibration experiences create a feedback loop. The more you dwell in these negative emotions, the more of these lower-frequency experiences you attract, which in turn reinforces the emotional state you're in. This is why it can feel difficult to escape a bad day or a negative mindset. You're trapped in a frequency that perpetuates the very struggles you're trying to avoid.

High-Vibration Experiences: The Power of Love, Joy, and Peace

On the other hand, when you are in a state of love, joy, or peace, your energetic frequency increases. These higher vibrational states resonate with positive, life-affirming energies, attracting experiences that match the higher frequency—opportunities for growth, abundance, and harmony in your life.

When you vibrate at a higher frequency, you open yourself to experiences that promote well-being and expansion. You might notice that things seem to flow more easily when you are in a state of joy or peace. New opportunities, meaningful connections, and moments of synchronicity tend to appear with greater frequency. This is because you energetically align with the higher frequencies of love and abundance, and thus, you attract more experiences that mirror these states.

For example, when you're feeling joyful, it's easier to see the positive in situations, and this mindset attracts positive outcomes. People are drawn to your energy, opportunities come your way, and challenges seem less daunting. In a state of love, your interactions with others tend to be more harmonious, and relationships thrive.

You naturally attract more support, understanding, and compassion from those around you.

Operating from a place of peace allows you to maintain a sense of calm, even in the face of adversity. Peaceful energy dissolves resistance, allowing solutions to flow effortlessly into your awareness. When you are at peace, you are open to the flow of life, and you begin to see opportunities for growth in every experience, no matter how challenging it might initially seem.

At higher vibrations, you become a magnet for abundance in all its forms—whether that's financial prosperity, fulfilling relationships, or personal growth. Life reflects the energy you project, and when that energy is rooted in love, joy, or peace, the universe responds in kind, bringing more experiences that resonate with those higher frequencies.

The key to transforming your life is learning to shift your energy from low- to high-vibration states. While it's natural to experience fear, anger, or frustration at times, the goal is to acknowledge those emotions without staying stuck in them. By becoming aware of your emotional state, you can consciously raise your vibration through gratitude, meditation, or simply focusing on the things that bring you joy.

When you start operating from a higher vibration, the shift in your energy field allows you to attract experiences aligned with your highest good. You move from a space of struggle and resistance into a state of flow, where opportunities, abundance, and harmony naturally find their way into your life.

Understanding this connection between your energy and experiences allows you to take control of your reality. By focusing on raising your vibration, you begin to shift your external world to match the elevated energy you are putting out.

More Energy than Physical

While we experience ourselves as solid, tangible beings, modern science—and ancient spiritual teachings—agree that at a fundamental level, we are composed of energy. The atoms that make up your body are mostly empty space, with tiny particles of energy in constant motion. The same is true for everything in the universe. The physical world, as we perceive it, is just a dense form of energy.

Seeing yourself as more energy than physical opens the door to a new way of living. You realize that:

Your thoughts are energy—The thoughts you think carry energy, and these energetic thought patterns influence your reality. Positive, uplifting thoughts raise your vibration, while negative, fear-based thoughts lower it.

Your emotions are energy—Emotions are powerful energetic forces that shape how you interact with the world. Emotional energy can get stuck in your body, affecting your vibration and physical health. Releasing and processing emotions in a healthy way can free up your energy and allow your vibration to rise.

Your actions carry energy—The actions you take in your life reflect your inner energy. When you act out of alignment with your highest self, your energy becomes scattered and fragmented. But when your actions align with your truth, your energy flows smoothly, and you feel empowered and centered.

In essence, the more you recognize your energetic nature, the more control you have over the flow of your life.

Raising Your Vibration

One of the most important concepts in understanding energy is that your vibrational frequency is not static—it can rise or fall depending on your thoughts, emotions, and actions. To raise your vibration is to align yourself with higher energy frequencies, which opens the door to greater experiences of peace, abundance, and spiritual connection.

Why Raise Your Vibration?

When you raise your vibrational frequency, several things happen:

- You naturally attract higher vibrational experiences into your life, such as positive relationships, fulfilling work, and joyful opportunities.

- You begin to interact with higher dimensional beings—guides, angels, or other entities who exist at higher frequencies than your everyday reality. These beings can assist you in your personal growth, offering wisdom, guidance, and support.

- Your perspective expands, allowing you to see the bigger picture of life. You begin to recognize the interconnectedness of all things and experience more synchronicities and moments of clarity.

- Your life flows more easily. When you are in alignment with higher energies, you experience less resistance. Problems that once seemed overwhelming become manageable or even disappear.

How to Raise Your Vibration

Mindful thoughts—Focus on cultivating positive, loving, and compassionate thoughts. This doesn't mean ignoring challenges but instead choosing thoughts that empower you rather than ones that keep you stuck in fear or doubt.

Emotional balance—Practice emotional regulation, allowing yourself to feel and process emotions without being overwhelmed by them. Meditation, journaling, and breathwork can help clear stuck emotional energy.

Energy work—Practices like Reiki, acupuncture, and energy healing can help to remove energetic blockages and restore the natural flow of energy in your body.

Connect to nature—Spending time in nature helps to ground and elevate your energy. Nature is in constant harmony with higher frequencies, and being in it can help you realign your vibration.

The Evolution of Humanity: Flow or Resistance

We are currently in a period of profound, energetic evolution. As the planet itself raises its frequency, humanity is being called to evolve as well. Whether you realize it or not, you are part of this evolutionary process. The question is: are you in the flow, or are you resisting?

Evolution is happening no matter what. You cannot stop this shift, but you can choose how you move through it. Those who embrace the changes, allowing their vibration to rise and their consciousness to expand, will find the transition smoother. They will experience life as a flow, moving with the current of evolution rather than fighting against it.

However, if you are resisting—clinging to old patterns of fear, scarcity, or separation—this evolutionary process can feel uncomfortable. It may manifest as physical, emotional, or mental distress as your system tries to adapt to the higher frequencies.

The key to flowing with this evolution is learning to calm and relax your nervous system, allowing you to integrate the incoming energies more easily.

Relaxing the Nervous System and Returning to Neutral

As you evolve and hold more energy, your body changes significantly. The nervous system, the bridge between the physical and energetic bodies, is particularly sensitive to these shifts. When your nervous system is in a state of fight or flight, it becomes difficult for you to integrate higher frequencies.

Learning to calm and relax the nervous system is crucial for this integration. When the nervous system is neutral, your body becomes more receptive to holding higher vibrations. Practices like deep breathing, meditation, and grounding exercises can help return the nervous system to balance, creating the space needed for your energetic evolution to unfold smoothly.

Activating Your Latent DNA

As your vibrational frequency increases, something remarkable happens at the cellular level. You start to activate your latent DNA. Much of our DNA is still considered "junk" by mainstream science, but it is increasingly believed that this dormant DNA holds incredible potential, particularly as we evolve into higher states of consciousness.

As you raise your vibration, you may begin to access latent abilities such as heightened intuition, telepathy, or a deeper connection to universal wisdom.

Your body is evolving to hold more light and energy. This process may come with physical symptoms as your cells adapt, but it ultimately results in a more harmonious and energetic system.

By activating your latent DNA, you are aligning with the higher vibrations of the universe and unlocking the blueprint of your fullest potential.

Understanding that you are energy is the foundation of conscious evolution. By raising your vibration, calming your nervous system, and embracing the natural changes in your body, you step into the flow of evolution, where life becomes a rich, harmonious dance of energy and experience.

In the next chapter, we'll explore what standing in your creator energy means and deeper practices to harness this newfound understanding of energy to manifest the reality you truly desire.

CHAPTER 8

YOU ARE THE CREATOR OF YOUR REALITY

At the core of your existence lies a powerful truth: you are the creator of your reality. Every thought, emotion, and belief you hold shapes the world you experience. You are not merely a passive observer of life, waiting for things to happen to you—you are an active participant, constantly creating your reality with every decision you make, every intention you set, and every belief you choose to embody. The experiences you see around you largely reflect your inner state of being.

In this chapter, we will explore what it means to stand in your creator energy. We'll delve into the power of love and compassion as the foundation of creation, the oneness that unites us all, and how to step into the higher vibrational experience of the New Earth Timeline.

Remembering Your Power

Many people have forgotten the immense creative power they hold within themselves. Conditioned by societal norms, external expectations, and old belief systems, it's easy to assume that life is happening *to* you rather than *through* you. The truth is that you create your reality by the energy you put out into the world. You are a co-creator with the universe, and you shape your life experience every day.

To step into this awareness requires that you remember your power. This power is not about controlling external circumstances but recognizing that your inner world—the energy, beliefs, and intentions you cultivate—directly influences your experience in the outer world.

Many people create unconsciously, allowing their thoughts and emotions to run on autopilot. They react to life's events rather than intentionally directing their energy. However, once you realize that you have the power to consciously choose your thoughts, emotions, and beliefs, you begin to align your inner world with the reality you want to experience.

Every moment presents an opportunity to make a choice—how you respond, what you focus on, and what energy you bring to a situation. By becoming more conscious of these choices, you can create a life that reflects your highest desires and purpose.

When you stand in this creator energy, you recognize that your power comes from within, and the reality you experience directly reflects the energy you are projecting.

Standing in Your Creator Energy with Love and Compassion

At the heart of true creation lies two fundamental energies: love and compassion. These are the highest vibrational frequencies in the universe, and when you create from a place of love and compassion, you align with the most powerful forces in existence. Creation born from love is expansive, uplifting, and harmonious, while creation driven by fear or scarcity leads to contraction, struggle, and conflict.

Why Love and Compassion?

Everything in the universe is made from the energy of love. When you create from love, you align with the fundamental nature of reality. Love expands, heals, and brings things into balance. When you hold love in your heart as you create, your reality reflects that harmony.

Compassion allows you to connect deeply with yourself and others. It softens your perception of the world, dissolves judgment, and encourages understanding. When you stand in your creator energy with compassion, you recognize that every being is on their unique journey, and you honor that journey with kindness. Compassion shifts the energy from separation to unity, allowing you to create from a place of interconnectedness.

When you bring love and compassion into your creative process, you create a reality that aligns with your desires and contributes positively to the collective whole.

The Basis of Everything Is Love

Love is the foundation upon which the entire universe is built. It is not just an emotion or feeling but an energy that permeates everything, from the smallest particles of matter to the vastness of space. The basis of everything is love.

Love is the energy that holds the universe together. It is the force that fuels creation and evolution. When you align with the energy of love, you tap into the infinite potential of the universe. This allows you to manifest and create in ways that resonate with your highest self.

Fear is often the biggest barrier to stepping fully into your creator energy. It contracts, limits, and keeps you stuck in old patterns. But love is the antidote to fear. When you choose love, you shift your vibration, opening yourself to greater possibilities and higher timelines.

By choosing to see the world through the lens of love, you create a reality that reflects that choice. Love becomes the lens through which you perceive yourself, others, and the world around you.

We Are All One—The Unity of Consciousness

At the deepest level, we are all connected. Every being, every soul, and every part of creation is interconnected through the fabric of energy that makes up the universe. We are all one. This oneness means that when you create, you are not only affecting your individual reality, but you are also influencing the collective experience.

In our physical world, we often see ourselves as separate individuals, living separate lives. But this is an illusion. At the quantum level, we are all connected through a unified energy field. This means that the energy you put into the world affects your personal life, ripples out, and influences the collective consciousness.

When you create from love, you contribute to elevating the collective energy. As more people awaken to their creative power and align with love, the collective vibration of humanity rises. This collective shift is part of the evolution of consciousness that we are currently experiencing.

Understanding this unity invites you to approach creation as an individual act and a contribution to the whole. When you create with love, you uplift not only your reality but the realities of those around you.

Experiencing the New Earth Timeline

As humanity undergoes this energetic evolution, we are moving into the New Earth Timeline, a higher vibrational reality where unity, love, compassion, and peace are the foundations of life. The New Earth represents a shift in consciousness, where individuals awaken to their creative power and collectively create a world that reflects these higher values.

What Is the New Earth Timeline?

The New Earth Timeline is a reality that exists at a higher frequency and is available to those who choose to align with it. It is a timeline of harmony, where humanity has moved beyond fear, separation, and conflict. In this timeline, love is the guiding force, and individuals live in alignment with their highest purpose and potential.

To experience the New Earth Timeline, you must first shift your inner vibration to match it. This means raising your frequency through love, compassion, and conscious creation. As more individuals make this shift, the New Earth Timeline becomes more accessible to the collective, and we begin to experience a reality that is more peaceful, joyful, and connected.

What Timeline Do You Choose?

At every moment, you are choosing which timeline to experience. The reality you see before you directly results from your energetic choices—your thoughts, emotions, beliefs, and actions. What timeline do you choose?

Live consciously—To choose the timeline that best reflects your highest desires, you must become a conscious creator. This means being aware of the energy you are emitting and choosing thoughts, beliefs, and actions that align with love, abundance, and peace.

Align with your highest self—Your highest self always exists in the timeline that reflects your greatest potential. By aligning with your highest self—through love, compassion, and conscious creation—you can enter that timeline and experience a reality that resonates with your soul's purpose.

Choose the New Earth Timeline—As you raise your vibration and align with love, you naturally gravitate toward the New Earth Timeline. You make this conscious choice every day by the energy you put into the world.

You are the creator of your reality. By standing in your power, creating from a place of love and compassion, and consciously choosing the timeline you wish to experience, you not only transform your personal life but also contribute to the collective evolution of humanity.

What you focus on creates your reality, and the timeline you choose determines the life you will live. The New Earth is calling—will you choose to step into it?

In the next chapter, we will explore how the power of love conquers fear and how it shifts us into higher-frequency consciousness.

LOVE AS THE KEY TO HIGHER CONSCIOUSNESS

At the deepest level of our existence, we are all connected—both to one another and to the infinite source of life. Separation is an illusion, a byproduct of the polarized reality we experience in the third and fourth dimensions. When we move beyond the illusion of separation and understand the fundamental truth that we are one, everything begins to shift. We realize that love is the force that unites us and is, in fact, the essence of who we truly are. Love is the energy that binds us to each other and to Source, and through love, we raise our vibration and step into higher dimensional reality.

In this chapter, we will explore the power of love to dissolve fear, the role of unconditional love in transforming our relationships and our world, and how love shifts us into a higher frequency of consciousness. By embracing love as the basis of our existence, we naturally transcend the limitations of fear and move into a reality of peace, unity, and expanded awareness.

The Illusion of Polarization and Separation

From the moment we are born into this world, we are conditioned to believe in separation. We learn to see ourselves as distinct individuals, separate from one another, from nature, and from Source. This sense of separation creates fear, isolation, and competition, leading to feelings of scarcity and disconnection.

However, this perception of separation is not the ultimate reality. At the most fundamental level, everything in the universe is interconnected through the energy of Source. Just as the waves are inseparable from the ocean, so too are we inseparable from one another and from the divine energy that animates all life.

The recognition that "I am you, and you are me" comes from understanding that we are all aspects of the same Source energy, expressing itself in different forms. While our experiences and perspectives may differ, the essence of who we are is the same. This shared essence is love, the energy of creation itself.

We are not only connected to each other but also to the Source from which we all originate. This divine energy, often referred to as Source, God, or the Universe, flows through everything and unites all existence. When we remember this connection, we realize that we are never alone and that the love of Source is always available.

Disco Ball Example

Imagine a disco ball suspended in the center of a vast room, shimmering with light. This disco ball represents Source, the infinite energy of creation, oneness, and consciousness. Each of the mirror pieces on the ball's surface symbolizes an individual human soul—a unique expression of Source energy. While reflecting different aspects of the light, these pieces are all intricately connected, forming a harmonious whole.

Each mirror piece on the disco ball represents a different person, each looking out from their unique perspective, or "window," into the world. The light that shines from each person reflects their consciousness and experience, and as they shine, they cast beams of light onto the ground, representing the lives they live and the realities they create.

The pieces of mirror that are closer together on the disco ball have a similar view. These individuals might share similar experiences, beliefs, or understandings about the world. They perceive reality in ways that are somewhat aligned, seeing similar truths and having comparable experiences. These individuals may feel connected because their perspectives are more closely aligned, and their light reflects similarly into the world.

However, the mirror pieces that are farther apart have completely different views. They reflect different aspects of the same light and look out through different windows. These individuals may have experiences, beliefs, or truths that seem foreign or contradictory to those with a closer perspective. Yet, despite these differences, they are still part of the same Source: the same disco ball.

This variety of perspectives represents the diverse experiences we see in the third-dimensional polarized reality. People living on opposite sides of the disco ball may feel disconnected from one another because their views and experiences seem so vastly different. However, from a higher perspective, these individuals simply look at the world from different angles, each reflecting a unique piece of the whole.

When you look at the lights hitting the ground, it appears as though each light is separate from the others. These lights represent the individual realities each person is experiencing. From the perspective of standing on the ground, it seems like each light is isolated, just as in our everyday lives, it often seems we are separate from one another. We experience different events, hold different beliefs, and lead different lives. This perception of separation creates the illusion that we are all alone, cut off from one another, existing in our independent realities.

But if you trace the lights back to their origin, something profound becomes clear. Despite their different appearances on the ground, all the lights come from the same Source—the disco ball. There is no true separation. What appeared to be isolated beams of light, representing different people and perspectives, are all expressions of the same unified energy source. They are interconnected, part of the same whole, even though they reflect outward in different directions.

This metaphor helps explain the polarized reality we experience in the third-dimensional world. In our everyday lives, it seems like people's perspectives are often at odds with one another. Some see the world one way, while others see it differently. This polarization creates conflict, division, and the sense that one person's truth might invalidate another's. But just as all the lights from the disco ball are part of the same Source, all perspectives are valid for those experiencing them.

Each person looks out from their own "window" of consciousness, shaped by their life experiences, beliefs, and soul journey. From their viewpoint, their perspective is completely true and real. Someone standing on the opposite side of the disco ball may have a vastly different perspective that contradicts the first person's reality, but that doesn't make either perspective less valid. Both are true within the context of their own experience.

When viewed from a higher dimension or a more expanded consciousness, the differences in perspective dissolve into unity. Just like the disco ball is a unified whole despite its many facets, humanity is one—a collection of individual expressions of the same Source energy. The experience of polarity and separation is a necessary part of the third-dimensional reality, allowing for growth, evolution, and the discovery of unity beyond difference.

In essence, this metaphor reminds us that there is no real separation. What we see as different, separate, or conflicting simply reflects the angle from which we view the world. If we shift our awareness to a higher perspective, we can see that we are all part of the same Source, shining light in different directions but originating from the same center.

All perspectives are true within the context of the person experiencing them, and all of us are connected in the grand mosaic of life.

Love Is the Key to Transformation

Love is the most powerful force in the universe. It transcends time, space, and all dimensions. When you come from a place of love, you align yourself with the true essence of who you are. In this state of alignment, you will naturally rise into higher states of consciousness, where fear no longer governs your reality.

Why Is Love the Key?

Love is the force that dissolves the illusion of separation. When you love yourself and others unconditionally, you recognize the inherent oneness of all beings. Love creates a sense of unity and interconnectedness, reminding us that we are all part of the same divine energy.

The vibration of love is one of the highest frequencies in the universe. When you live from a place of love—love for yourself, love for others, and love for life—you naturally raise your energetic vibration. This elevated state of being allows you to step into higher dimensional realities, where peace, harmony, and joy are the dominant frequencies.

Fear is a product of the belief in separation. When you believe you are separate from others and Source, you may experience fear—fear of loss, failure, and the unknown. However, love is the antidote to fear. When we know that we are connected to each other and to Source, we realize there is nothing to fear. Even death loses its power when you understand that your energy and consciousness live on beyond the physical body.

Loving Ourselves to Love Others

Self-love is the foundation of all love. To truly love others unconditionally, you must first come to a place of fully loving and accepting yourself. Self-love is not about ego or selfishness; it is about recognizing your inherent worth as a divine being and treating yourself with kindness, compassion, and respect.

When you love yourself, you can heal the wounds of judgment, guilt, and shame that have kept you disconnected from your true essence. As you embrace self-love, you let go of the limiting beliefs and fears that have held you back and open yourself to experiencing the fullness of life.

When you come from a place of self-love, you no longer need to judge or criticize others. Your ability to love others unconditionally flows naturally when you have healed the parts of yourself that once felt unworthy or unlovable. You can begin to see others as reflections of yourself, recognizing that we are all on the same journey of growth and expansion.

By loving yourself, you raise your vibration and open the door to loving others without conditions or expectations. This unconditional love is transformative both for you and the world.

Shifting Into a Higher Dimensional Reality Through Love

As you raise your vibration through love, you naturally shift into a higher dimensional reality where love, unity, and peace are the dominant experiences. In this state, you are free from the lower vibrational energies of fear, judgment, and separation, and you can begin to experience life from a higher perspective.

Love is the bridge that carries us from lower vibrational realities, where fear and duality dominate, into higher dimensional states of being. When you consistently choose love over fear, you align yourself with higher timelines where love is the guiding force. These higher timelines are characterized by peace, harmony, and a deep sense of interconnectedness with all life.

One of the key shifts that occurs as you move into a higher dimensional reality is the transition from living in the mind to living in the heart. The heart is the center of love and compassion, and it is through the heart that you access higher states of consciousness. By practicing heart-centered awareness and allowing love to guide your decisions, you naturally raise your vibration and shift into a more expansive reality.

Moving Beyond Fear

Fear is the primary obstacle to experiencing higher consciousness. Fear arises from the belief that we are separate from each other, from Source, and from our true selves. It manifests as anxiety, worry, judgment, and the desire to control or protect ourselves from perceived threats.

However, when we know that we are always connected to Source and that our true nature is eternal, fear begins to lose its grip on us. The realization that there is nothing to fear opens the door to greater freedom and peace.

One of the deepest fears many people carry is the fear of death. This fear is rooted in the belief that death is the end of our existence. However, when we understand that our energy and consciousness live on beyond the physical body, the fear of death dissipates. We recognize that death is simply a transition from one state of being to another and that our soul's journey continues.

Similarly, many people fear the unknown—whether that's the future, change, or uncertainty. But when we live from a place of love and trust in our connection to Source, we realize that we are always supported and guided, no matter what challenges arise. Love helps us confidently embrace the unknown, knowing everything unfolds in divine timing.

Embodying Love to Shift the Collective Consciousness

As more of us choose to live from a place of love, we begin to shift not only our individual reality but the collective consciousness as well. The more we embody love, the more we contribute to elevating the collective frequency. This creates a ripple effect, helping others awaken to their capacity for love and oneness.

As you continue to raise your individual vibration through love, you naturally inspire others to do the same. Your energy affects those around you, and when you live from love, you help to dissolve the collective fear, judgment, and separation that have dominated the world for so long.

The more people who embody love and unity, the more we collectively shift into a new reality based on higher dimensional principles of love, compassion, and oneness. This is the process of creating the New Earth, where love is the foundation of all interactions and humanity lives in harmony with each other and the planet.

As you embrace love as the basis of who you are, you will naturally shift into a reality of peace, unity, and higher consciousness.

In the next chapter, we will explore practical techniques for amplifying your creative energy, deepening your connection to your higher self, and manifesting the life you desire in alignment with the highest timeline.

SECTION II

Tools And Techniques
For Shifting Timelines

AMPLIFYING YOUR CREATIVE ENERGY AND DEEPENING YOUR CONNECTION TO YOUR HIGHER SELF

Now that you have developed the awareness and tools to stay aligned with your highest timelines, the next step is to expand your creative energy and deepen your connection to your higher self. These practices will help you tap into your full creative potential and manifest your desired life, fully aligned with the highest version of yourself. By increasing your creative power and strengthening your relationship with your higher self, you can more easily navigate timelines and bring your dreams into reality.

In this chapter, we'll delve into practical techniques to enhance your creative energy, strengthen your connection to your higher self, and apply these practices to manifest a life aligned with your highest potential.

Amplifying Your Creative Energy: The Foundation of Manifestation

Your creative energy is the force that brings your desires, goals, and dreams into reality. It is the fuel that powers your ability to manifest your ideal timeline. By amplifying this energy, you increase your capacity to create and shape your reality more easily and precisely.

Movement is one of the most effective ways to amplify your creative energy. Physical movement helps clear stagnant energy, allowing new inspiration and ideas to flow more freely. Practices like yoga, dance, tai chi, or even simple stretching help activate the body's creative centers, clearing energetic blocks and creating space for new possibilities. Make regular movement a part of your daily routine to keep your creative energy flowing.

Breathwork is another powerful tool for amplifying creative energy. Conscious breathing practices, such as pranayama or deep diaphragmatic breathing, help increase the flow of energy throughout your body and clear any mental or emotional stagnation that may be limiting your creativity. When you breathe deeply and with intention, you increase your connection to life force energy (or prana), which fuels your creative potential.

- Try this simple breathwork practice: Sit comfortably, close your eyes, and take slow, deep breaths. Inhale for a count of four, hold for four, exhale for four, and hold again for four (a practice known as box breathing). Focus on filling your entire body with energy as you breathe in, and visualize releasing any blockages as you exhale.

Once your creative energy is amplified, it's important to tap into the flow state—the space where ideas, inspiration, and solutions arise effortlessly. Set aside time for activities that help you enter this flow state, whether it's writing, painting, problem-solving, or another creative endeavor. The more you cultivate moments of flow, the easier it becomes to access your creative potential and use it to manifest your highest timeline.

Deepening Your Connection to Your Higher Self

Your higher self is the aspect of you that exists beyond the physical realm, operating from a place of infinite wisdom, love, and understanding. Deepening your connection to your higher self allows you to access greater guidance, insight, and alignment with your true purpose. This connection is essential for manifesting in alignment with the highest timeline, ensuring that your desires are in harmony with your soul's path.

Meditation deepens your connection to your higher self. By quieting the mind and turning inward, you open the door to receive guidance and insight from this higher aspect of yourself. Set aside time each day to meditate with the intention of connecting to your higher self. You can visualize a light above your head—representing your higher self—pouring down guidance and love as you meditate.

Another way to deepen your connection to your higher self is through journaling. Set the intention to communicate with your higher self, and then begin to write. Start by asking a question or seeking clarity about a situation, and allow your higher self to respond through your writing. This process can be incredibly revealing, as it helps you access wisdom and insight you may not be consciously aware of.

- You can try prompts like, "What is my next step toward manifesting my highest timeline?" or "What do I need to release to fully align with my soul's purpose?"

Your intuition is the voice of your higher self, guiding you in real time. To strengthen your connection to this inner guidance, practice listening and acting on your intuitive nudges. The more you trust and follow your intuition, the stronger your connection to your higher self becomes. Intuitive guidance often appears as subtle feelings, "gut instincts," or synchronicities in your external world. Pay attention to these signals and trust that your higher self is leading you toward your highest timeline.

Manifesting with Intention: Aligning with Your Highest Timeline

Once you've amplified your creative energy and deepened your connection to your higher self, it's time to focus on the practical steps for manifestation. Manifestation is the process of bringing your desires into reality, and when done in alignment with your highest self, it leads to fulfilling your soul's purpose.

The first step in manifestation is to set clear and specific intentions. What do you want to create? What timeline are you aligning with? Be as specific as possible in defining your goals and desires, as clarity helps the universe bring your vision into reality. Write down your intentions and revisit them regularly, ensuring that they reflect your true desires.

Visualization is a powerful manifestation tool because it trains your mind to align with your desired timeline. When you visualize, imagine your goal as already achieved. Picture the details, feel the emotions, and immerse yourself in the experience of having already stepped into that reality. The more you practice visualization, the more you align your energy with the timeline you wish to create.

Manifestation is not only about focusing on your desires—it also requires taking inspired action. Your higher self will guide you toward opportunities, choices, and actions that align with your desired outcome. Listen to your intuition and follow through on the steps it leads you toward, even if they feel small or insignificant. Action aligns energy, and when you take action that is in harmony with your intention, you accelerate the manifestation process.

One of the most important aspects of manifestation is to release attachment to how your desires will come to fruition. Trust that the universe will bring about your desired outcome in the best possible way, even if it doesn't unfold exactly as you imagined. By letting go of control, you allow the universe to work in alignment with your highest good, often delivering results that are even better than you expected. Think about it in terms of "this or something better."

Practical Tools for Staying Aligned with Your Manifestation Process

To stay aligned with your manifestation process, it's important to use practical tools that help keep your focus and energy directed toward your desired outcomes. These tools can help you stay on track, maintain your vibration, and ensure that you are continuously moving toward your highest timeline.

Affirmations are powerful statements that help reprogram your subconscious mind and align your energy with your desired reality. Write down positive affirmations that reflect your goals and repeat them daily. Examples might include:

"I am aligned with my highest timeline."

"Abundance flows easily into my life."

"I trust my higher self to guide me toward my dreams."

Consistent use of affirmations helps strengthen your belief in your ability to manifest.

Vision boards are visual representations of your goals and desires. By creating a vision board filled with images, words, and symbols that represent your highest timeline, you keep your focus on what you want to manifest. Place your vision board somewhere you will see it daily, and use it as a reminder of your intentions and the timeline you are aligning with.

Practicing gratitude for what you already have and the outcomes you create helps maintain a high vibrational alignment with your desired timeline.

Each day, write down or reflect on the things you are grateful for, both in your current life and the future reality you are manifesting. Gratitude amplifies your creative energy and strengthens your connection to the timeline where your desires come to fruition.

It's important to stay grounded in the present moment, especially when working on manifesting your highest timeline. Grounding practices, such as walking barefoot on the earth, spending time in nature, or practicing mindfulness, help you stay centered and balanced as you create your desired reality. Grounding also prevents burnout and keeps your energy stable as you work toward your goals.

By incorporating these practices—meditation, visualization, intention setting, and inspired action—you can access greater creative power, clarity, and alignment with your soul's purpose.

As you move forward, remember that manifestation is a dynamic process that requires both inner alignment and external action. By amplifying your energy, trusting your higher self, and taking practical steps toward your goals, you will continuously move toward the timeline that reflects your highest potential.

In the next chapter, we will look at practical, actionable steps you can take to consciously shift your timeline and create the life you desire.

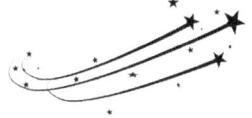

CHAPTER 11

PRACTICAL TECHNIQUES FOR CONSCIOUSLY NAVIGATING TIMELINES

Now that we understand the quantum nature of time—that all timelines exist simultaneously and that we are not bound by the past or an inevitable future—it's time to explore how to harness your focus and intention to consciously navigate timelines. By mastering these techniques, you can begin to live from a place of empowerment, actively choosing the reality you want to experience.

In this chapter, we'll explore practical, actionable steps to intentionally shift your timeline and build the life you envision. Practicing these techniques consistently will deepen your ability to move into higher vibrational realities that align with your highest potential.

Living in the Now: The Importance of the Present Moment

Understanding that all timelines exist simultaneously leads to a powerful realization: the only reality that truly exists is the one you are experiencing right now. The past is merely a memory, and the future is a possibility. However, the present moment is where all potential realities intersect. This is where you hold the greatest power to influence your life.

By living in the present and becoming aware of your choices, thoughts, and emotions, you can consciously shape the trajectory of your life and step into the timeline that reflects your deepest desires. This chapter combines the understanding of living in the present moment with practical techniques to help you become a conscious creator of your reality.

Many spiritual traditions emphasize the importance of being fully present. When you live in the present, you are not weighed down by regrets from the past or anxieties about the future. Instead, you actively participate in the creation of your reality. The present moment is where you choose your timeline, where all potential realities are available, and where you can collapse possibilities into a lived experience.

Your ability to influence your life begins with an understanding that everything happens in the present. Every choice, decision, and thought you make in the present moment determines which timeline you experience. When you are fully present and conscious of your thoughts and actions, you gain control over your reality. This is the essence of conscious creation.

Aligning with Your Desired Reality

In the quantum field, infinite possibilities exist at once. The timeline you experience reflects where you focus your attention and energy. To live a life of abundance, joy, love, and fulfillment, you must align your thoughts and actions with those qualities. The present moment is where you have the most power to shape your future.

Each moment allows you to align with the timeline that reflects your highest life vision. For example, if you desire more love in your relationships, focus on embodying love, compassion, and understanding in the present. By doing this, you collapse potential timelines and step into the reality where those experiences are more likely to manifest.

One of the most effective ways to shift timelines is to embody the energy of the reality you wish to experience. Act as though you are already living that life. If you desire success, confidence, and abundance, align your thoughts, behaviors, and emotions with that outcome. By embodying the qualities of the timeline you want to experience, you create a vibrational match that draws that reality to you.

Shifting timelines is not always immediate, but it is happening constantly. As you focus on new possibilities and direct your energy toward creating the reality you want, trust in the process. The universe responds to your energy, even if changes are subtle at first. Focus on your desired reality and remain open to how it may unfold—even if it doesn't happen exactly as you imagined.

Freedom from the Past and Future

One of the greatest gifts of understanding the quantum nature of time is the realization that you are no longer constrained by the past or an inevitable future. The past is not set in stone, and the future is not predetermined. Both are fluid and shaped by the choices you make in the present.

Release attachment to the past—Since all timelines exist simultaneously, your past is not fixed. You can reframe or heal past experiences by shifting your focus. The emotional energy you carry from past events can be released when you recognize that those experiences represent only one version of reality. By shifting into a new timeline, the past loses its power to influence your present, and you gain the freedom to create a new narrative.

Create your future—The future is equally fluid and responsive to your current focus and energy. It is not something that "happens" to you; it is something you create through your current actions and thoughts. By consciously directing your energy toward the desired outcomes, you begin to shape the future timeline you will experience. What you focus on now becomes the foundation of your future.

Clarifying Your Vision

The first step in navigating timelines is to clarify the vision of the life you want to create. You cannot shift into a new reality if you are unclear about what that reality looks or feels like. Clarity is essential because your focus and intention collapse the quantum field of possibilities into your lived experience.

Spend time visualizing the reality you want to create. What does it look like? How do you feel in this reality? What kind of experiences are you having? The clearer your vision, the easier it becomes to align your focus with that timeline. Visualization is a powerful tool because it engages your emotions and imagination, key elements in creating your desired reality.

Writing down your vision helps solidify it in your mind and energy field. Describe your ideal life in detail, as if it is already happening. Use the present tense to bring the vision into the now. For example, "I live in a state of joy and abundance. I wake up each day feeling fulfilled and excited about my work. My relationships are loving and supportive."

While it's important to be clear on the specific details of your vision, the most powerful aspect of creation is the feeling state you wish to experience. Ask yourself: How do I want to feel in this new reality? Whether it's love, peace, excitement, or abundance, focusing on the emotions you want to cultivate will help you align your vibration with the timeline that supports those feelings.

Setting Intentions

Once you have a clear vision, the next step is to set powerful intentions. Intentions act as the guiding force that directs your focus toward the timeline you want to experience. They serve as an energetic signal to the universe, aligning your energy with your desired outcome.

When setting intentions, be as specific as possible. Rather than saying, "I want to be happy," try something more concrete, like, "I intend to live each day with joy, gratitude, and inner peace." Avoid using negative language like "I don't want to be stressed," because the universe responds to the energy behind your words, and focusing on stress may bring more of it. Instead, reframe it positively: "I intend to live with ease and flow."

Intentions are most powerful when you reinforce them daily. Set aside time each morning to declare your intentions for the day. You can say them out loud, write them down, or simply hold them in your mind during meditation. This consistent practice helps anchor your focus in the timeline you want to experience.

Once you set your intentions, release any attachment to how or when they will manifest. Trust that the universe is aligning things perfectly behind the scenes. Your role is to hold the vision and remain open to how it unfolds.

Practicing Conscious Focus

Where your attention goes, energy flows. This is the core principle behind consciously navigating timelines. Your focus is the key that unlocks the potential of any timeline, and practicing conscious focus helps you stay aligned with your desired reality.

One of the most effective ways to practice conscious focus is through mindfulness. Throughout your day, pay attention to where your thoughts are going. Are you focusing on worry, fear, or lack? Or are you focusing on gratitude, love, and possibility? Gently redirect your focus whenever you catch yourself spiraling into negative thought patterns.

Since time is not linear, the present moment is your point of power. Make it a habit to anchor your attention in the now. Meditation, breathwork, and grounding exercises are excellent tools for cultivating present-moment awareness. The more grounded you are in the present, the easier it becomes to consciously choose where to direct your focus.

The thoughts you focus on will shape the timeline you experience. Whenever you notice disempowering thoughts, replace them with empowering ones. For example, if you catch yourself thinking, "I'm not good enough," shift it to, "I am capable and deserving of success." This conscious redirection helps you align with timelines where you realize your highest potential.

Embodying the Energy of Your Desired Timeline

It's not enough to simply think about the timeline you want to experience—you must embody the energy of that reality in the present moment. By aligning your emotions, thoughts, and actions with the energy of your desired outcome, you collapse the potential into reality.

Feel as if it's already here. This is one of the most powerful ways to shift timelines. Spend time each day feeling the emotions of your desired reality, as if it's already happening. How would you feel if you were living the life you envision? Cultivate those emotions in your body. By consistently generating the emotional frequency of your desired timeline, you attract that reality into your experience.

While thoughts and emotions are powerful tools for navigating timelines, action grounds those shifts into the physical world. Take steps that align with the reality you want to experience. For example, if your vision involves a career change, start taking action toward that goal—researching new opportunities, networking, or acquiring new skills. Every action that aligns with your vision moves you closer to that reality.

Practice gratitude. Gratitude is one of the highest vibrational frequencies, and practicing it daily helps anchor you in higher timelines. Even if your desired reality hasn't fully manifested yet, express gratitude for where you are and what you already have. Gratitude shifts your focus away from lack and aligns you with abundance, making it easier to step into a timeline of fulfillment.

Releasing Resistance and Limiting Beliefs

Often, the biggest obstacle to shifting timelines is the resistance created by limiting beliefs and old patterns. These beliefs act like energetic anchors, keeping you tied to a timeline that no longer serves you. To shift into a new reality, you must release the beliefs and resistance holding you back.

Start by identifying the beliefs that may be keeping you stuck. These could be beliefs about yourself (e.g., "I'm not good enough"), about life (e.g., "Life is hard"), or about others (e.g., "People can't be trusted"). Once you've identified these beliefs, ask yourself where they came from and whether they truly serve you.

Once you're aware of your limiting beliefs, begin to challenge them. Are they really true? Could there be another way of looking at the situation? Reframe the belief in a way that supports your desired reality. For example, if you've believed that "Money is scarce," reframe it to "The universe is abundant, and I am always supported."

Resistance often comes from holding onto old hurts, grudges, or guilt. Forgiveness is a powerful tool for releasing resistance and freeing yourself to move into a new timeline. Forgive yourself for past mistakes, and forgive others for any harm they've caused. This releases the energetic hold that those past experiences have on you and opens the door to new possibilities.

Trusting the Process of Creation

Navigating timelines is not always an instantaneous process. Shifts may take time to manifest fully in the physical world, and it's important to trust the process as it unfolds. The universe is always responding to your energy, and as you maintain your focus and intention, you will begin to see signs of alignment with your desired reality.

As you align with a new timeline, you may notice synchronicities— meaningful coincidences that act as signs from the universe. These can be subtle nudges that you are on the right path, or they may come in the form of new opportunities, unexpected encounters, or moments of clarity.

Hold the vision, even in challenges. Sometimes, challenges arise just before a major shift occurs. These challenges may be opportunities to release old patterns or beliefs that no longer serve you. Stay committed to your vision, even in the face of difficulty. Trust that every experience is part of your journey toward the timeline you are consciously choosing.

Stay open to unexpected outcomes. While a clear vision is important, remain open to the idea that the universe may have something even greater in store for you. Stay flexible and allow your desired timeline to unfold unexpectedly, knowing that the universe always works for your highest good.

By clarifying your vision, setting intentions, practicing conscious focus, and embodying the energy of your desired reality, you can step into the timeline of your choosing. Releasing resistance and limiting beliefs while trusting the process helps anchor your shift into the physical world.

In the next chapter, we will explore how to sustain these practices in daily life, maintaining alignment with higher timelines and creating lasting change in your reality. By building a strong foundation of focus, intention, and trust, you can continuously evolve into higher frequencies of existence.

CHAPTER 12

SUSTAINING TIMELINE SHIFTS AND CREATING LASTING CHANGE

Now that you've learned the techniques for consciously navigating timelines, the next step is to integrate these practices into your daily life to ensure lasting change. Aligning with higher timelines requires consistency, dedication, and a strong foundation of focus, intention, and trust. This chapter will explore how to maintain that alignment in the face of daily challenges and distractions and build practices that help you continuously evolve into higher frequencies of existence.

When you choose to shift timelines, the journey doesn't end with the initial shift. It's an ongoing process of alignment and realignment, where you strengthen your connection to the reality you desire and release anything that pulls you back into lower vibrational states. The key is to stay committed to the process, even when the external world presents challenges or triggers old patterns.

Establishing Daily Rituals to Maintain Focus

One of the most effective ways to sustain alignment with your desired timeline is by establishing daily rituals that help maintain your focus and intention. These rituals serve as anchors, grounding you in the energy of your chosen timeline and helping you stay connected to your vision.

Set a morning intention—Each morning, take a few minutes to reconnect with your vision and set intentions for the day. This practice reminds you of the timeline you choose to align with and helps you direct your energy toward that reality. You can do this through meditation, visualization, or journaling. Ask yourself, "What do I want to focus on today? How do I want to feel? What energy do I want to embody?"

Mindful check-ins throughout the day—Throughout the day, check in with yourself to see if you are staying aligned with your intentions. Are you still focused on your desired outcome, or have you been pulled into distractions, stress, or negativity? Mindful check-ins help you course-correct in real time, bringing your attention back to your vision and aligning you with higher vibrational timelines.

Evening reflection and gratitude—Before bed, reflect on your day. How well did you stay aligned with your intentions? What went well, and where did you get off track? Express gratitude for the progress you made and the lessons learned. This practice helps you close the day positively and sets the tone for continued alignment the next day.

By incorporating these simple rituals into your daily routine, you strengthen your ability to stay focused on your desired reality and maintain the energy of your chosen timeline.

Staying Aligned in the Face of Challenges

It's natural to encounter challenges as you navigate timelines, especially when old patterns, beliefs, or circumstances arise that seem to pull you back into lower vibrations. The key to sustaining higher timelines is to approach these challenges with awareness and use them as opportunities for growth.

Observe without attachment—When challenges arise, observe them without becoming emotionally attached. Rather than reacting from fear or frustration, take a step back and view the situation as an observer.

Ask yourself, "What is this challenge showing me? How can I respond in a way that aligns with my higher self?" This practice helps you stay centered and prevents you from slipping into old patterns.

Stay committed to your vision—In moments of difficulty, it can be tempting to revert to familiar, lower vibrational states. However, staying committed to your vision is crucial for aligning with your chosen timeline. When challenges arise, remind yourself of your intentions and the reality you are creating. Trust that the challenge is part of your growth and that you will move through it with greater ease by staying aligned.

Use challenges as stepping stones—Every challenge presents an opportunity to release old energies and patterns that no longer serve you. When you encounter resistance, fear, or doubt, recognize that these energies can be transmuted. Use the challenge as a stepping stone to a higher timeline, knowing that by moving through it, you are strengthening your alignment with your desired reality.

Building a Strong Foundation of Trust

Trust is a crucial component in sustaining higher timelines. Trusting the creation process, trusting yourself, and trusting the universe to support your intentions are all essential for creating lasting change. Without trust, it's easy to fall into doubt or impatience, which can pull you out of alignment.

Not everything manifests immediately; sometimes, your desired reality may take time to unfold in the physical world. Trust that everything is happening in divine timing and that the universe is aligning things perfectly for your highest good. Stay patient and open, knowing your timeline shift is in progress, even if it hasn't fully materialized.

You are a powerful creator who can shape your reality through your focus and intention. Trust in your creative power and know you can manifest the life you desire. If doubt arises, reaffirm your belief in yourself and remind yourself of past successes where you consciously created positive outcomes.

While it's important to have a clear vision and intention, there is also a need to surrender control over how things unfold. Trust that the universe often knows the best way to bring your desires into reality and that things may not always happen exactly as you expect. Stay open to the possibilities and remain flexible, allowing the universe to guide you toward the timeline that serves your highest good.

Releasing Old Patterns to Maintain Higher Timelines

As you align with higher timelines, you may notice that old patterns, beliefs, and behaviors no longer resonate with your new reality. To maintain your alignment with higher frequencies, it's important to release these old energies so that they no longer hold you back.

Identify patterns that no longer serve you. Take time to reflect on the patterns in your life that no longer align with the reality you want to create. This could be thought patterns, habits, or even relationships rooted in fear, scarcity, or limitation. Once you've identified them, acknowledge that these patterns have served their purpose and are ready to be released.

One of the most effective ways to release old patterns is through forgiveness—of yourself and others. Holding onto guilt, shame, or resentment keeps you tied to lower vibrational timelines. By practicing forgiveness, you free yourself from the past and open space for new, higher vibrational experiences.

As you release old patterns, consciously choose new patterns that align with your higher timeline. This could mean adopting new beliefs, behaviors, or relationships that reflect your new reality. For example, if you're releasing a scarcity mindset, replace it with a practice of abundance—whether through affirmations, gratitude, or acts of generosity.

Surrounding Yourself with Supportive Energy

Your external environment plays a significant role in aligning with higher timelines. Surrounding yourself with supportive energy—whether in the form of people, environments, or activities—can help you stay grounded in your chosen reality.

Curate your environment—Create a physical environment that reflects the energy of your desired timeline. This could mean decluttering your space, adding elements that inspire peace or creativity, or incorporating symbols and reminders of your intentions. Your environment should uplift and support you as you align with higher frequencies.

Choose supportive relationships—Surround yourself with people who support your growth and alignment with higher timelines. These people uplift you, encourage your vision, and resonate with the energy you are embodying. Be mindful of relationships that drain your energy or pull you into old patterns of fear or judgment.

Engage in activities that raise your vibration—Consistently engage in activities that help raise your vibration and align you with higher frequencies. This could include meditation, yoga, nature walks, creative pursuits, or anything that brings you joy and peace. Regularly engaging in high-vibrational activities strengthens your alignment with your desired reality.

Creating Lasting Change Through Consistency

The most important factor in sustaining alignment with higher timelines is consistency. Lasting change doesn't happen overnight; it requires regular practice and dedication. The more consistent you are with your focus, intentions, and energy, the more deeply you anchor yourself in your desired reality.

Make alignment with higher timelines a daily practice, not something you do sporadically. Whether through morning rituals, mindful check-ins, or regular meditation, make it a habit to realign yourself with your desired reality each day.

Celebrate small shifts. As you continue to align with higher timelines, celebrate the small shifts and signs of progress. Every step toward your desired reality is a victory; acknowledging these shifts reinforces your alignment. Gratitude for each small success helps you maintain momentum.

Stay patient and persistent. Lasting change takes time, and it's important to stay patient and persistent. There may be moments when it feels like nothing is happening, but trust that every action you take, every thought you shift, and every intention you set is moving you closer to your desired reality. Persistence is key to maintaining higher timelines.

By staying consistent in your focus, intention, and actions, you can create lasting change and continue to evolve into higher frequencies of existence.

In the next chapter, we will explore how to maintain alignment in relationships, work, and the world around you, integrating higher vibrational living into all aspects of your life. By mastering these practices, you will transform your reality and inspire and uplift those around you.

CHAPTER 13

MAINTAINING ALIGNMENT IN RELATIONSHIPS, WORK, AND THE WORLD AROUND YOU

As you continue to align with higher timelines and consciously create your desired reality, the challenge becomes integrating this new way of being into all aspects of your life. Maintaining alignment in relationships, work, and your external environment is key to creating a life that reflects your highest potential. By embodying higher vibrational energy in every area of your life, you not only transform your reality but also inspire and uplift those around you.

This chapter will explore maintaining alignment while interacting with others, navigating your career or work environment, and engaging with the broader world. By mastering these practices, you can grow and expand while helping others do the same.

Maintaining Alignment in Relationships

Relationships are one of the most significant areas where your alignment with higher timelines will be tested. Whether it's family, friends, romantic partners, or colleagues, the people you interact with reflect different levels of consciousness, which can sometimes challenge your ability to stay grounded in higher vibrations. However, your relationships also offer a powerful opportunity for growth and the expansion of love, compassion, and understanding.

Be mindful of energy dynamics. Every relationship involves an exchange of energy. Some people lift you up and help you stay aligned with your higher self, while others may drain your energy or pull you into old patterns of judgment, fear, or negativity. Consciously choose how much time and energy to invest in each relationship. Surround yourself with people who support your growth and bring positive energy into your life.

Set energetic boundaries. It's important to set healthy boundaries to maintain your alignment. This doesn't mean cutting people off or withdrawing from relationships, but rather learning to protect your energy and stay centered in your own vibration. If certain people bring stress, negativity, or conflict into your life, set clear boundaries that allow you to stay in your higher vibration while still engaging with them from a place of love and compassion.

When conflicts arise or others challenge your growth, respond from a place of love and understanding rather than reacting with fear or defensiveness. Take a moment to ground yourself and observe the situation from a higher perspective. Ask yourself, "How can I respond in a way that aligns with my higher self? What can I learn from this interaction?" By choosing to respond with patience, empathy, and understanding, you help to raise the vibration of the relationship itself.

Lead by example. As you embody higher vibrational energy, you naturally become an example for others. You influence people by the energy you bring to your relationships. When you remain calm, centered, and focused on love and compassion, it encourages those around you to rise to that same vibration. When you lead by example, you inspire others to do the same.

Aligning with Higher Frequencies in Work and Career

Work and career are areas where many people feel challenged to stay aligned with their higher self. The demands of deadlines, performance pressures, and workplace dynamics can pull you into lower vibrations of stress, competition, or fear. However, shifting your perspective can bring your higher vibrational self into your work life, creating a more harmonious and fulfilling experience.

One of the most important ways to stay aligned at work is to ensure that your career or work aligns with your values and sense of purpose. When your work reflects your core values, you naturally feel more fulfilled and motivated, and it becomes easier to maintain a higher vibration. If you feel that your current work is out of alignment with your values, consider ways to adjust your approach or seek out opportunities that resonate more deeply with your soul's purpose.

Even if your work is demanding or stressful, you can shift the energy of your day by bringing mindfulness to each task. Focus on the present moment and approach your work with intention and care. This practice helps you to stay grounded, reduce stress, and bring more flow into your daily routine. Mindfulness also allows you to access creative solutions and see challenges from a higher perspective.

Just as in your personal relationships, the energy dynamics of your work-place relationships play a significant role in your ability to stay aligned. Seek to build positive, supportive connections with your colleagues and clients, and be mindful of the energy you bring into these interactions. When conflicts or challenges arise, approach them with empathy and a willingness to find common ground.

Before you start your workday, set an intention for how you want to feel and what energy you want to bring to your work. This could be an intention to stay calm and focused, approach your tasks creatively, or bring more kindness and collaboration to your workplace. By setting energetic intentions, you align yourself with a higher frequency and create a workday that reflects that energy.

Navigating the World from a Higher Vibration

Living in alignment with higher timelines doesn't mean disconnecting from the world around you—it means engaging with the world from a higher perspective. Whether navigating social media, watching the news, or engaging in your community, it's important to stay grounded in your energy and avoid being pulled into the collective fear, division, or negativity that often dominates the public sphere.

Filter what you consume—The information you consume—whether it's news, social media, or entertainment—directly impacts your energy and vibration. Be discerning about the content you engage with and choose sources that uplift and inspire you. If certain content makes you feel fearful, anxious, or angry, it's important to step back and redirect your focus to higher vibrational information.

Observe without attachment—It's easy to get emotionally attached to the events happening in the world, especially regarding issues of injustice, conflict, or suffering. However, staying emotionally attached to these events can lower your vibration and pull you into timelines of fear or disempowerment. Practice observing the world from a higher perspective, understanding that all events are part of the larger evolution of consciousness. You can hold compassion for the world without being consumed by its challenges.

Engage with intention—If you engage with world events, do so from a place of intention and purpose. Rather than reacting emotionally or feeling overwhelmed, ask yourself how you can contribute positively to the situation. Whether volunteering, donating, or simply sending love and positive energy, engaging with the world from a place of intention helps you stay aligned with higher frequencies while making a meaningful impact.

Inspiring and Uplifting Others Through Your Alignment

As you maintain your alignment with higher timelines, you become a powerful force for positive change, not only in your own life but in the lives of those around you. Your energy influences others, and by embodying love, compassion, and higher consciousness, you inspire others to do the same.

As you grow and expand, share your experiences and insights with others. Whether through conversation, social media, or creative expression, your story can inspire those around you to explore their potential for growth. Vulnerability and authenticity are key here—by being open about your challenges and triumphs, you create a space for others to reflect on their journeys.

Just as you are on your path of growth and alignment, so are others. Hold space for their journey without judgment, understanding that everyone is evolving at their own pace. Offer support, encouragement, and love as they navigate their timeline shifts, and trust that they are exactly where they need to be.

Your alignment has a ripple effect on the world around you. When you embody higher frequencies, you naturally raise the vibration of your environment, relationships, and community. Even small acts of kindness, love, and compassion can profoundly impact the people you interact with, helping them align with higher timelines as well.

Living in Alignment as a Continuous Journey

Living in alignment with higher timelines is not a one-time shift; it is a continuous journey of growth, expansion, and realignment. There will be moments when you feel deeply connected to your higher self, and there will be moments when you feel challenged or pulled into old patterns. The key is to stay committed to the process and trust that every step forward, no matter how small, is part of your evolution.

Take time to celebrate the progress you've made. Every shift in consciousness, every moment of growth, and every step toward your desired reality is a victory. Acknowledging your progress helps reinforce your alignment and motivates you to keep moving forward.

As you navigate higher timelines, remember to be gentle with yourself. Growth is not always linear, and there may be times when you feel like you're slipping back into old patterns or struggling to maintain alignment. Practice self-compassion during these times, knowing that every experience is an opportunity for learning and expansion.

As you continue to align with higher timelines, stay open to the infinite possibilities the universe has in store for you. Your journey is not fixed or limited—new opportunities, relationships, and experiences are always unfolding. Trust that the universe is constantly guiding you toward your highest good.

By staying mindful of your energy, responding from a place of love, and creating positive, supportive environments, you can continuously align with higher frequencies and inspire those around you to do the same.

CHAPTER 14

EXPANDING YOUR UNDERSTANDING OF MULTIDIMENSIONAL EXISTENCE AND DEEPENING YOUR CONNECTION TO YOUR HIGHER SELF

As you continue your journey of conscious timeline navigation and higher vibrational living, the next step is to expand your understanding of your multidimensional existence and deepen your connection to your higher self. In doing so, you gain access to even higher levels of consciousness, clarity, and empowerment, allowing you to step more fully into your role as a conscious creator of your reality.

Understanding Your Multidimensional Nature

We are more than just physical beings living in a three-dimensional reality. You are a multidimensional being, existing simultaneously in multiple dimensions of consciousness. The part of you that you perceive as your physical self is only one aspect of your full, expansive being. In higher dimensions, your soul expresses itself in ways that go beyond the limitations of physical reality, and by accessing these higher dimensions, you can tap into greater wisdom, love, and understanding.

What Does It Mean to Be Multidimensional?

Being multidimensional means that you exist on many levels of consciousness, from the physical dimension you are currently aware of to higher dimensions where time, space, and physical limitations no longer apply. These higher aspects of yourself are always present, guiding you, and you can access them by expanding your awareness and raising your vibration.

Your higher self is the aspect of you that exists in these higher dimensions, serving as a bridge between your physical reality and the greater aspects of your soul. It holds the blueprint of your soul's purpose, guiding you through your life experiences and helping you navigate the complexities of multidimensional existence. Deepening your connection to your higher self allows you to access the wisdom, clarity, and insight needed to align with your highest timeline.

Deepening Your Connection to Your Higher Self

Connecting with your higher self is one of the most powerful ways to access higher levels of consciousness and deepen your understanding of your multidimensional nature. Your higher self is always available to you, and by cultivating a conscious relationship with it, you can tap into its guidance, love, and wisdom more easily.

Meditation and stillness—One of the most effective ways to deepen your connection to your higher self is through meditation. In stillness, you quiet the mind and allow the voice of your higher self to come through. A regular meditation practice helps you tune into the subtler aspects of your being, making it easier to access your higher self's guidance. Begin each meditation by setting the intention to connect with your higher self and allow yourself to relax into that connection.

Journal as a dialogue with your higher self—Another powerful tool for connecting with your higher self is journaling. Create space each day to write down any questions or concerns, and allow your higher self to respond through your writing. The more you practice this form of dialogue, the more naturally the wisdom of your higher self will flow through. Over time, you'll begin to recognize the distinct voice of your higher self guiding you toward clarity and understanding.

Heart-centered awareness—The heart is often referred to as the seat of the soul, and it's through the heart that we access higher dimensions of consciousness. By bringing your awareness to your heart center, you can deepen your connection to your higher self. Practice focusing on your heart throughout the day, breathing deeply and imagining a radiant light expanding from your chest. This practice opens you to the unconditional love and wisdom of your higher self.

Expanding Your Consciousness Beyond the Physical Realm

To fully embrace your multidimensional nature, you must expand your consciousness beyond the limitations of the physical realm. This means learning to see yourself as more than just a body, more than just a mind, and more than just the sum of your physical experiences. Expanding your consciousness allows you to access higher frequencies of energy and wisdom, giving you a greater understanding of the interconnectedness of all things.

Tap into the quantum field—The quantum field is the space where all possibilities exist simultaneously. By expanding your consciousness into this field, you can access the infinite potential of the universe and consciously choose which timelines, experiences, and realities you want to align with. Practices such as quantum visualization or quantum jumping can help you access this field and shift into new levels of reality. In quantum visualization, you imagine yourself stepping into the version of reality you desire, feeling the energy and emotions of that timeline as if it's already happening.

Explore higher dimensions through visualization—Visualization is a powerful tool for exploring higher dimensions of consciousness. Spend time visualizing yourself in expanded states of awareness, where you are free from the limitations of the physical world. You might imagine yourself surrounded by light, traveling through galaxies, or connecting with higher dimensional beings. These visualizations help you attune to higher frequencies and expand your awareness beyond the physical realm.

Channel higher wisdom—Channeling is a process where you allow the wisdom and energy of higher dimensional beings or your higher self to flow through you. Whether through writing, speaking, or creative expression, channeling allows you to receive insights beyond your conscious mind. To channel, enter a meditative state and set the intention to connect with your higher self or a higher dimensional guide. Trust what comes through, even if it doesn't make logical sense at first, and allow yourself to receive the wisdom meant for you.

Accessing Higher Levels of Consciousness

As you deepen your connection to your higher self and expand your awareness into higher dimensions, you begin to access higher levels of consciousness. These elevated states allow you to see beyond the limitations of duality and separation, accessing a greater sense of unity, love, and interconnectedness with all life.

Experience unity consciousness—Unity consciousness is the understanding that all beings, experiences, and realities are interconnected and part of the same divine source. As you raise your vibration and expand your consciousness, you begin to experience this deep sense of oneness with everything around you. In this state, fear, judgment, and separation dissolve, and you can move through life with greater compassion, love, and understanding.

Live from a higher perspective—When you access higher levels of consciousness, you naturally view life from a higher perspective. You are no longer caught up in the drama and limitations of the physical world but can observe your experiences from a place of detachment and understanding. This higher perspective allows you to make decisions from a place of wisdom rather than reacting from fear or limitation.

Transcend the illusion of time—In higher states of consciousness, the illusion of linear time begins to dissolve. You experience time as a fluid, multidimensional reality where past, present, and future coexist. This expanded awareness allows you to access wisdom from your past experiences, receive guidance from your future self, and align more fully with the present moment.

Stepping Into Your Role as a Conscious Creator

As you deepen your understanding of your multidimensional existence and strengthen your connection to your higher self, you begin to step more fully into your role as a conscious creator. You realize that you are not just a passive participant in life but an active co-creator with the universe, shaping your reality through your focus, intention, and vibration.

When you are connected to your higher self and aligned with higher levels of consciousness, you create from a place of alignment. This means that your creations are in harmony with your soul's purpose and infused with the energy of love, abundance, and expansion. When you create from this space, the universe responds by aligning circumstances, opportunities, and people to support your vision.

One of the most important aspects of being a conscious creator is trusting your creative power. As you expand your consciousness, you understand that your thoughts, intentions, and energy shape your reality. Trust that you have the power to create the life you desire and that the universe is always supporting you in bringing your vision into physical form.

While your thoughts and intentions are powerful, it's through inspired action that you bring your creations into reality. Inspired action is action that aligns with your higher self and your vision for your life. It feels effortless, exciting, and expansive. When you act from a place of alignment, you are in the flow of creation, and the universe supports you in manifesting your desires.

By cultivating a relationship with your higher self, tapping into higher dimensions of consciousness, and creating from a place of alignment, you can unlock new levels of potential and transformation in your life.

In the next chapter, we will explore how to integrate the wisdom of higher consciousness into your daily life, ensuring that you remain grounded while accessing expanded states of awareness.

CHAPTER 15

INTEGRATING HIGHER CONSCIOUSNESS INTO DAILY LIFE

As you expand your awareness and connect more deeply with higher levels of consciousness, the next challenge is learning how to integrate that wisdom into your daily life. Accessing higher states of consciousness allows you to tap into greater insights, love, and purpose, but the key to creating lasting transformation is learning how to apply that wisdom to the everyday moments of your life. By balancing the spiritual and the physical, you can live a life of purpose, love, and mastery while staying grounded in your present reality.

In this chapter, we will explore practical ways to integrate higher consciousness into the rhythm of your daily routines, relationships, work, and personal growth. Doing so allows you to connect deeply to your higher self and spiritual wisdom while thriving in the material world.

Grounding Yourself in the Present Moment

Staying grounded is one of the most important aspects of integrating higher consciousness into daily life. When you access expanded states of awareness, it's easy to feel detached from the physical world or disconnected from the responsibilities of daily living. However, the true mastery of spiritual wisdom comes from bringing that higher awareness into the present moment.

Daily grounding practices—Regular grounding practices help you stay connected to both the Earth and your higher self. You can ground yourself by spending time in nature, walking barefoot on the earth, practicing breathwork, or doing physical exercises like yoga. These activities help anchor your energy into the physical world, creating a stable foundation for higher awareness.

Mindful presence—Practice bringing mindful awareness into all of your daily activities. Whether cooking, working, or engaging with others, focus on being fully present in the moment. This helps you bridge the gap between the spiritual and the material, allowing you to experience each moment as an opportunity for growth and expansion.

Balancing higher awareness with practical action—While staying connected to higher consciousness is important, it's equally important to stay grounded in practical reality. Balance your spiritual insights with tangible action in the world. If you receive guidance from your higher self, take the necessary steps to implement that wisdom in your daily life. This balance between awareness and action is key to mastering your reality.

Living from a Place of Love and Compassion

Higher states of consciousness naturally align you with the frequencies of love and compassion. When you access higher awareness, you begin to see the interconnectedness of all life and understand that love is the essence of everything. Integrating this wisdom into your daily life means living from a place of love and compassion in all your interactions and choices.

Choose love in every moment—As you go about your day, consciously choose to act from a place of love. Whether it's how you speak to yourself, interact with others, or approach your work, allow love to guide your actions. This simple shift in intention raises your vibration and infuses your daily life with positive energy.

Compassion for others—Higher consciousness reveals the oneness of all beings. Seeing others through this lens makes it easier to practice compassion, even toward those who may challenge you. Recognize that everyone is on their own journey, and extend empathy and understanding to those around you. This approach helps you stay aligned with higher vibrations, even in difficult situations.

Self-love and acceptance—Integrating higher consciousness into your daily life also means practicing deep self-love and acceptance. As you become more aware of your multidimensional nature, you realize that every aspect of yourself—your strengths, flaws, and experiences—is part of your growth. Embrace yourself fully, knowing you are always evolving toward greater love and understanding.

Bringing Higher Awareness Into Your Work and Purpose

Integrating higher consciousness into your work allows you to align your career and life purpose with the wisdom of your higher self. When you approach your work from a place of alignment and higher awareness, you naturally bring more creativity, flow, and meaning into what you do. Whether in a spiritual profession or a more traditional career, you can infuse your work with the energy of your higher self.

Reflect on whether your work aligns with your higher self's purpose. If your career feels out of alignment, consider how to bring more meaning and intention into your work. This might mean shifting your focus within your current role, pursuing a new career path, or incorporating more of your spiritual gifts into your work. The more aligned you are with your higher purpose, the more fulfilled and inspired you will feel daily.

No matter what you do for work, you can infuse it with higher awareness. Before starting your day, take a moment to connect with your higher self and set an intention to bring love, creativity, and purpose into your tasks. This practice helps you stay aligned with your spiritual wisdom while engaging with the physical world.

Higher consciousness reveals that we are all here to serve one another in various ways. Reflect on how your work can serve others, whether through direct impact or by contributing to a greater cause. When you approach your work as a form of service, you elevate its purpose and align more deeply with the energy of love and compassion.

Cultivating Conscious Relationships

Your relationships are one of the most powerful areas where you can integrate higher consciousness. When you interact with others from a place of higher awareness, you bring more harmony, understanding, and depth to your connections. Conscious relationships are those in which both individuals are committed to growth, love, and mutual respect.

Conscious communication is about speaking and listening from a place of love, respect, and awareness. When you communicate with others, be fully present and listen deeply. Speak from your heart and express yourself with clarity and kindness. This practice fosters greater connection and understanding in your relationships.

In conscious relationships, both people are growing and evolving. Allow space for your partner, friends, and loved ones to be on their own journey, without trying to control or change them. Offer support and love, but recognize that everyone has their own path to follow. This approach nurtures a sense of trust and respect in your relationships.

True intimacy is built on vulnerability and authenticity. In your relationships, practice being open about your feelings, thoughts, and experiences. Share the wisdom you've gained through your connection to higher consciousness, and encourage those around you to do the same. Vulnerability creates deeper connections and helps both you and others grow.

Finding Balance Between the Spiritual and the Physical

The key to living a life of mastery is finding a balance between your spiritual insights and the physical world. It's important to stay connected to higher consciousness while also honoring the responsibilities and experiences of the material world. Finding this balance allows you to live a grounded and expansive life where spiritual wisdom is fully integrated into your everyday experience.

While it's important to access higher states of consciousness, it's equally important to honor your physical experience. Your body is a vessel for your soul's growth and is vital in your spiritual journey. Take care of your physical body through nourishment, movement, and rest, recognizing that your physical well-being supports your spiritual growth.

Spirituality doesn't need to be separate from your everyday life. Rather than seeing your spiritual practice as something you do apart from the rest of your life, look for ways to bring spirituality into everything you do. Whether through mindful breathing, gratitude, or loving-kindness, you can weave spiritual practices into every aspect of your life.

Higher consciousness often brings moments of profound stillness and peace, but life also requires action and engagement with the world. Find a balance between moments of stillness, where you connect with your higher self, and moments of action, where you apply that wisdom in the physical world. This balance allows you to move through life with both grace and purpose.

By balancing the spiritual with the physical, living from love and compassion, and bringing higher awareness into your relationships, work, and routines, you can live a life of purpose, love, and mastery.

In the next chapter, we will explore how to maintain your alignment with higher consciousness over the long term, navigating the ups and downs of life while continuing to grow and evolve. By staying committed to your path, you can ensure that your connection to higher consciousness remains strong and transformative throughout your life journey.

CHAPTER 16

MAINTAINING ALIGNMENT WITH HIGHER CONSCIOUSNESS OVER THE LONG TERM

Once you have established a connection to higher consciousness and begun to integrate its wisdom into your daily life, the next challenge is maintaining that alignment over the long term. Life is full of ups and downs, unexpected challenges, and periods of growth that may push you to your limits. To stay aligned with higher consciousness throughout these fluctuations, it's essential to develop practices and mindsets that keep you connected to your higher self, no matter what life brings.

Embracing Life's Cycles and Transitions

Life naturally moves in cycles—there are times of growth, expansion, and abundance, as well as periods of contraction, rest, and challenge. One of the keys to maintaining alignment with higher consciousness is learning to embrace these cycles without losing your connection to your higher self.

Honor the ebb and flow—Just as the seasons change, so too does your personal journey. There will be moments when you feel deeply connected to higher consciousness, and others when you feel more disconnected or challenged. Honor the ebb and flow of these cycles and trust that each phase has a purpose. Periods of challenge often bring opportunities for deeper growth and self-reflection, while moments of expansion allow you to integrate that growth.

Stay grounded during transitions—During times of transition, whether it's a career change, relationship shift, or personal transformation, it's easy to feel ungrounded or overwhelmed. In these moments, return to your grounding practices—whether through meditation, spending time in nature, or breathwork. Staying grounded helps you remain centered in your higher self, even when the external world feels uncertain.

Surrender and trust the process—Maintaining alignment with higher consciousness requires a deep level of trust in the process. Surrender to the flow of life, knowing that every experience leads you toward greater wisdom and understanding. Even when things don't go as planned, trust that your higher self and the universe are guiding you toward the highest possible outcome.

Cultivating Resilience and Emotional Mastery

One of the greatest challenges to maintaining alignment with higher consciousness is navigating emotional ups and downs. Humans experience a wide range of emotions, from joy and love to fear, anger, and grief. Navigating your emotions with resilience and emotional mastery is key to staying aligned with higher frequencies.

Allow emotions to flow—Resilience doesn't mean suppressing your emotions; it means allowing them to flow through you without becoming attached to them. When you experience difficult emotions like fear or anger, acknowledge them, allow yourself to feel them fully, and then let them go. This practice of emotional flow prevents you from getting stuck in lower vibrations and helps you return to alignment with your higher self.

Practice emotional self-regulation—Emotional mastery comes from self-regulating your emotional responses. When a challenging situation arises, take a moment to pause, breathe, and reflect before reacting. Ask yourself, "How can I respond to this situation from a place of love and awareness?" By choosing your emotional response consciously, you stay connected to higher consciousness, even in difficult circumstances.

Turn challenges into growth opportunities—Every emotional challenge is an opportunity for growth. When you face difficult emotions, ask yourself what lesson or insight your higher self is guiding you to learn. Growth often comes from the moments that push you out of your comfort zone. By embracing these challenges as opportunities for evolution, you strengthen your alignment with higher consciousness.

Staying Committed to Your Spiritual Practices

Consistency in your spiritual practice is crucial for maintaining alignment with higher consciousness over the long term. It's easy to become complacent during periods of ease or to neglect your practices during times of stress. However, staying committed to your spiritual routine ensures you maintain a strong connection to your higher self, no matter what is happening in your life.

Establish a daily routine that keeps you connected to your higher self. Whether it's meditation, journaling, prayer, or energy work, make it a nonnegotiable part of your day. These practices are like spiritual "maintenance," helping you stay aligned with a higher consciousness even when life feels busy or chaotic.

Your spiritual needs may change over time, and adapting your practices to meet those needs is important. During times of challenge, you may need more grounding or emotional healing practices, while during periods of expansion, you may feel called to explore more advanced spiritual techniques. Allow your practice to evolve with you, and trust your intuition to guide you to the practices that will support your alignment.

There may be times when you feel disconnected from your higher self or stuck in lower vibrational states. When this happens, return to the basics of your spiritual practice. Focus on grounding, mindfulness, and self-care. Sometimes, the simplest practices are the most effective in bringing you back into alignment.

Maintaining Alignment in Relationships and Social Interactions

Your relationships significantly affect your ability to stay aligned with higher consciousness. Whether with family, friends, colleagues, or strangers, your interactions with others can support your growth or challenge your alignment. By navigating relationships with awareness, you can maintain your connection to higher consciousness while fostering love, understanding, and growth.

Surround yourself with people who support your spiritual growth and align with your values. These relationships lift you up, encourage you to stay aligned with your higher self, and offer love and understanding. Be mindful of relationships that drain your energy or pull you into lower vibrations. While you don't have to cut these relationships out, setting healthy boundaries is important to protect your energy.

Conflict is inevitable in relationships, but how you respond to it determines whether you stay aligned with higher consciousness or fall into lower vibrations. Approach conflict from a place of love and awareness, seeking to understand the other person's perspective rather than reacting with anger or defensiveness. By staying calm and compassionate, you raise the vibration of the interaction and open the door to resolution and healing.

As you continue to align with higher consciousness, your energy naturally influences those around you. Be a source of light for the people in your life, offering love, understanding, and support. Your alignment with higher frequencies can inspire others to explore their spiritual path and raise their vibration. Remember that your energy has a ripple effect, touching the lives of those around you in powerful ways.

Continually Expanding Your Consciousness

The journey of aligning with higher consciousness is a continuous one. As you grow and evolve, new levels of awareness become available to you, offering deeper insights and greater understanding. To maintain your alignment over the long term, it's important to stay open to continued expansion and never stop exploring the infinite possibilities of your multidimensional self.

Embrace lifelong learning—Approach your spiritual journey with the mindset of a lifelong learner. There is always more to discover, whether it's through new spiritual teachings, personal insights, or experiences of higher states of consciousness. Stay curious and open to new ideas, and allow your understanding of reality to continue expanding.

Explore new dimensions of your being—As you deepen your connection to higher consciousness, you may feel called to explore new dimensions of your being. This could include connecting with higher dimensional beings, exploring past or parallel lives, or experiencing new levels of spiritual awakening. Follow your intuition and allow yourself to explore the vastness of your multidimensional self.

Stay open to the unknown—Higher consciousness often brings a sense of knowing, but it's important to stay open to the unknown as well. There will always be mysteries and aspects of reality beyond your current understanding. Embrace the unknown with a sense of wonder and curiosity, trusting that as you continue to grow, new layers of awareness will reveal themselves to you.

Trusting Your Path and Purpose

Maintaining alignment with higher consciousness requires a deep level of trust in your path and purpose. Even when challenges arise or life takes unexpected turns, it's important to trust that you are always guided by your higher self and the universe toward your highest good.

Your higher self is always guiding you, offering insights, nudges, and intuitive feelings that help you stay aligned with your path. Trust your inner guidance even when it doesn't make logical sense or when external circumstances seem difficult. The more you trust and follow your inner guidance, the more aligned you become with your soul's purpose.

Spiritual growth is not a race; there is no set timeline for reaching certain milestones. Trust that your growth is unfolding in divine timing and that every experience, no matter how challenging, is part of your evolution. By staying patient and allowing your growth to unfold naturally, you remain aligned with the flow of higher consciousness.

Your soul came here with a unique purpose, and aligning with higher consciousness helps you fulfill that purpose. Stay committed to your path, even when the journey feels uncertain or challenging. By trusting in your purpose and remaining aligned with your higher self, you will continue to evolve and positively impact the world around you.

By embracing life's cycles, cultivating emotional mastery, staying committed to your spiritual practices, and trusting your path, you can ensure that your connection to higher consciousness remains strong and transformative throughout your life journey.

In the next chapter, we will reflect on the transformative power of living in alignment with higher consciousness and how this journey not only elevates your own life but also contributes to the collective evolution of humanity.

CHAPTER 17

THE TRANSFORMATIVE POWER OF LIVING IN ALIGNMENT WITH HIGHER CONSCIOUSNESS

This path of spiritual awakening, personal growth, and multidimensional awareness is transformative, not just on an individual level but also for the collective evolution of humanity. By aligning with higher consciousness, you are contributing to creating a new reality—one based on love, unity, and higher awareness.

This chapter will explore how your personal journey elevates your life and radiates outward, creating ripples of positive change that inspire and uplift others. Together, we are participating in the collective ascension of humanity, co-creating a future that reflects our highest potential.

The Personal Transformation of Living in Alignment

The decision to live in alignment with higher consciousness brings about a profound personal transformation. As you integrate spiritual wisdom into your daily life, deepen your connection to your higher self, and raise your vibration, you experience a new way of being rooted in love, peace, and purpose.

When you align with your higher self, your life becomes infused with clarity and purpose. You no longer feel lost or disconnected from your path, but instead, you move through life with a deep sense of knowing that everything you do is in alignment with your soul's mission. This clarity empowers you to make choices that support your growth and well-being.

Higher consciousness naturally brings you into a state of inner peace. Even in the face of challenges, you can remain centered and grounded, knowing that everything is unfolding for your highest good. This peace creates a sense of deep fulfillment, as you realize that true happiness comes from within and is not dependent on external circumstances.

As you continue to raise your vibration and live in alignment with higher consciousness, love and compassion become the guiding forces of your life. You begin to see yourself and others through the lens of unity, recognizing that we are all interconnected. This shift in perspective allows you to release judgment, fear, and separation, replacing them with love, understanding, and empathy.

The Ripple Effect of Personal Transformation

While your personal journey of alignment with higher consciousness elevates your life, it also creates a powerful ripple effect that influences those around you. As you embody higher vibrations, you naturally uplift others, inspiring them to explore their own potential and live in alignment with their higher selves.

Every thought, emotion, and action you take is a vibration that ripples out into the collective consciousness. When you choose to live from a placc of lovc, compassion, and awareness, you raise the collective vibration of humanity. Your personal alignment becomes a beacon of light that helps others awaken to their spiritual potential.

One of the most powerful ways you influence the world is simply by being an example of what it means to live in alignment with higher consciousness. As others witness your transformation—how you navigate life with grace, clarity, and love—they are inspired to explore their own spiritual path. You become a role model for living a life of purpose, peace, and fulfillment.

The love and compassion you cultivate within yourself ripple out into the world, touching the lives of others in ways you may not even realize. Whether it's through your relationships, work, or simple acts of kindness, your energy contributes to the creation of a more loving, unified reality. This ripple of love and unity can shift the collective consciousness and bring lasting change.

Contributing to the Collective Evolution of Humanity

Your journey of alignment with higher consciousness is not only transformative on a personal level—it is part of a larger process of collective evolution. Humanity is undergoing a profound shift in consciousness, moving from a reality based on fear, separation, and limitation to one rooted in love, unity, and higher awareness. By aligning with higher consciousness, you are playing an active role in this collective ascension.

Shift the collective paradigm—As more individuals awaken to their multidimensional nature and choose to live in alignment with higher consciousness, the collective paradigm begins to shift. We move away from old systems and structures that no longer serve us—those based on division, scarcity, and control   and co create a new reality that reflects our highest potential. Your personal transformation contributes to this collective shift, helping to anchor the energies of love, peace, and unity on Earth.

Create the New Earth—The concept of the New Earth refers to a higher dimensional reality where humanity lives in harmony with each other, nature, and the universe. This new reality is not a distant possibility—it is being created right now through our choices and the energy we embody. Every time you choose love over fear, unity over division, and awareness over ignorance, you are helping to manifest the New Earth.

Collective ascension through individual growth—The collective evolution of humanity is made possible by each person's individual growth and awakening. As you raise your vibration and align with higher consciousness, you create a pathway for others to do the same. Together, we lift the collective into higher frequencies, where love, compassion, and unity become the foundation of our shared reality.

Co-Creating a Reality Based on Love, Unity, and Higher Awareness

Together, we are co-creating a new reality that reflects the highest aspects of our souls and our shared purpose as multidimensional beings. This reality is not based on fear, competition, or separation but on love, unity, and higher awareness. As more people align with higher consciousness, we collectively bring this vision into existence.

Live in unity consciousness—Unity consciousness is the understanding that all beings, all experiences, and all realities are interconnected and part of the same divine source. As you embody unity consciousness in your daily life, you create a world where love, respect, and cooperation are the guiding principles. In this new reality, we no longer see ourselves as separate from one another but as unique expressions of the same universal energy.

Anchoring higher frequencies on Earth—As you continue to raise your vibration and live in alignment with higher consciousness, you are anchoring higher frequencies on Earth. These frequencies of love, light, and awareness help dissolve old patterns of fear, scarcity, and division, creating a more harmonious and abundant reality. By holding these higher frequencies, you are helping to create a world where peace, joy, and unity are the norm.

Collective transformation through love—At the core of this collective evolution is the energy of love. Love is the force that unites, heals, and elevates us to our highest potential. By living from a place of love in your life, you contribute to the collective transformation of humanity. Together, we are creating a reality where love is the foundation of all relationships, interactions, and systems.

The Journey Continues

It's important to remember that the path of alignment with higher consciousness is a lifelong journey. There will always be new levels of awareness to explore, new lessons to learn, and new growth opportunities. The process of spiritual evolution is continuous, and each step you take brings you closer to your highest potential.

Celebrate your growth—Take a moment to reflect on how far you've come. Celebrate the growth, wisdom, and transformation you've experienced on this journey. Each moment of alignment, each act of love, and each insight gained is a step toward living in your highest truth.

Stay open to new possibilities—As you continue on your path, stay open to the infinite possibilities of higher consciousness. Trust that the universe is always guiding you toward your highest good and that new levels of awareness and expansion are always waiting to be discovered.

The journey is the destination—Ultimately, the journey itself is the destination. The practice of living in alignment with higher consciousness is not about reaching a final goal but about continuously evolving, expanding, and deepening your connection to your higher self and the universe. Embrace the journey with curiosity, love, and gratitude, knowing each step brings you closer to embodying your true, multidimensional nature.

This journey elevates your life, while also contributing to the collective evolution of humanity. Together, we are creating a new reality based on love, unity, and higher awareness where peace, compassion, and interconnectedness guide our every choice and action.

As you move forward, remember that your alignment with higher consciousness is a gift to the world. By embodying love, compassion, and awareness in your daily life, you are helping to create a future where humanity thrives in harmony with itself, the Earth, and the universe. The journey continues, and your role as a conscious creator is more important than ever. Together, we are building a new Earth that reflects the highest potential of all beings.

In the next chapter, we explore how shifting your focus can lead to creating your personal heaven on Earth.

SECTION III

Ascending To Fifth-Dimensional Reality

CHAPTER 18

CREATING YOUR PERSONAL
HEAVEN ON EARTH

What you focus on creates your reality. This universal truth is at the heart of conscious creation and spiritual ascension. Every thought, feeling, and belief you hold shapes the world you experience. As you go about your day, it's important to consider: What are you focusing on? Where do you place your attention? Are you caught up in the drama of the third- and fourth-dimensional Earth experience, or are you consciously focusing on higher, more aligned realities?

In this chapter, we will explore how shifting your focus can lead to the creation of your personal heaven on Earth. By intentionally directing your attention toward joy, abundance, self-love, and compassion, you can elevate your vibration and move into a higher dimensional experience of reality. We will also look at how to let go of the old stories, beliefs, and relationships that no longer resonate with your new, higher frequency. Ultimately, you have the power to choose your timeline and create a different reality from those around you. The key lies in where you place your attention.

Where Is Your Attention?

Take a moment to reflect on where your attention goes throughout the day. Are you constantly consuming negative media, such as the news or social media that perpetuates fear and division? Do you find yourself getting caught up in the drama of everyday life, whether it's personal conflicts, societal problems, or sensational stories?

Whatever you give your attention to expands in your experience. When you focus on fear, scarcity, or conflict, you amplify those energies in your life. If your attention is constantly directed toward the chaos of the external world, you are likely to feel overwhelmed, anxious, and disconnected from your inner truth.

Much of the third- and fourth-dimensional Earth experience is based on duality and drama. It's easy to get pulled into the stories of good versus bad, right versus wrong, truth versus conspiracy. But this constant focus on external drama keeps you stuck in lower vibrational timelines, where fear and separation dominate. To shift out of this reality, you must consciously redirect your attention to higher frequencies of love, joy, and abundance.

Creating Your Personal Heaven on Earth

Now, imagine what your life could be like if you focused on creating your own heaven on Earth. What if you decided to place your attention on the things that bring you joy, peace, and fulfillment? How would your reality shift if you lived from a place of love and abundance?

Live in joy—Joy is one of the highest vibrational states you can experience. When you focus on activities, relationships, and experiences that bring you joy, you naturally elevate your vibration. What if you allowed yourself to play, explore your passions, and follow what lights you up? By focusing on joy, you create more of it in your life.

Believe in abundance—What if you knew, deep in your heart, that the universe is completely abundant and that there is more than enough for everyone? This belief shifts you from the scarcity mindset that dominates the third-dimensional world into a higher dimensional reality where abundance flows freely. When you place your attention on the abundance that surrounds you, you align yourself with that energy, attracting more of it into your life.

Practice self-love and acceptance—Self-love is the foundation of spiritual growth and ascension. When you focus on truly loving yourself and accepting all parts of who you are, you release the need for external validation or comparison. As you cultivate this deep self-love, you extend it to others, accepting them without judgment. Imagine how different your reality would be if you and everyone around you were fully accepted and loved unconditionally.

By focusing your attention on these higher vibrational experiences—joy, abundance, and love—you begin to create a personal reality that reflects these qualities. This is your personal heaven on Earth, a life where you fully align with your soul's purpose, and peace, harmony, and fulfillment are your everyday experience.

Ascending into the Fifth-Dimensional Experience

The fifth-dimensional experience is one of unity, love, and higher consciousness. As we ascend into this new reality, we leave behind the heaviness of third- and fourth-dimensional dramas and step into a lighter, more expansive way of being. The key to this ascension is focus—what you focus on determines which dimension you align with.

At your core, you are more energy than physical matter. As you raise your vibrational frequency by focusing on love, joy, and abundance, you become lighter. This lightness allows you to ascend into higher frequencies where fear, separation, and scarcity no longer exist. The more consistently you focus on higher vibrational thoughts and feelings, the more you anchor yourself in the fifth-dimensional experience.

The fifth dimension is heart-centered. It is a reality where love, compassion, and unity are the guiding principles. When you come from a place of love—love for yourself, love for others, love for life—you naturally raise your vibration. This shift in frequency allows you to move into higher dimensional timelines where fear no longer rules your reality.

Choosing and Staying in Your Desired Timeline

All timelines exist simultaneously, and you can choose which one you want to experience. The timeline you are on is a reflection of your focus and energy. When you consciously direct your attention toward higher frequencies, you shift into a new timeline that reflects your highest desires and aspirations.

To fully embrace a new timeline, you must let go of the old stories that no longer serve you. These stories are often rooted in fear, limitation, and separation, anchoring you in lower dimensional realities. Whether these stories are about your past, your identity, or your beliefs about what is possible, they must be released for you to step into a higher vibrational timeline.

As you raise your vibration, you may find that some relationships no longer align with your new frequency. This is a natural part of the ascension process. When you shift into a higher dimensional timeline, those not vibrating at the same frequency may fall away. This can be challenging, but it is necessary to maintain your alignment with the new reality you are creating.

To stay in your chosen timeline, it's important to consistently hold the vision of what you want to create. Feel the emotions of that reality as if it's already here. The more you live from this state, the easier it becomes to stay aligned with your new timeline. This doesn't mean that challenges won't arise, but your ability to stay focused on your higher vision will keep you anchored in the reality you want to experience.

Creating Your Own Reality Amidst Others

One of the most empowering aspects of timeline shifting is the realization that you can have a completely different experience than the person next to you. Even though we live in the same physical world, our individual realities are shaped by our focus and beliefs. As you elevate your vibration and shift into a higher dimensional timeline, your experience of life can be vastly different from those still focused on lower vibrational dramas.

Maintain your vibration in a world of contrast—It can be challenging to stay in a higher vibrational state when others around you are caught up in fear, conflict, or scarcity. However, by staying centered on your energy and focusing on love, joy, and abundance, you can maintain your alignment with your desired timeline. You don't have to be affected by the collective drama; instead, you can create your own reality, even amidst the contrast.

Influence the collective through your vibration—As you hold a higher vibration, you naturally influence those around you. Your energy becomes a beacon of light, and others may begin to shift their focus simply by being in your presence. This is how collective consciousness evolves—one person at a time raising their vibration and holding space for others to do the same.

By letting go of old stories and aligning with your desired timeline, you can live a completely different reality than those around you.

In the next chapter, we will explore how embracing your true nature as an energetic being can accelerate your spiritual ascension, enabling you to shift into higher dimensional realities.

CHAPTER 19

ASCENDING TO THE FIFTH-DIMENSIONAL EXPERIENCE AND CHOOSING YOUR TIMELINE

Our journey of spiritual evolution ultimately leads to the fifth-dimensional experience, where we recognize that we are more energy than physical matter. As we shed the dense layers of fear, judgment, and limiting beliefs, we become lighter—both in body and spirit. This lightness allows us to ascend into higher frequencies, aligning with timelines of greater love, joy, peace, and unity.

This chapter will explore how embracing your true nature as an energetic being can accelerate your spiritual ascension, enabling you to shift into higher dimensional realities. By letting go of old stories, limiting beliefs, and relationships that no longer resonate, you can consciously choose to live in the fifth dimension, where all possibilities exist and you align with your highest timeline.

Understanding the Fifth-Dimensional Experience

The fifth dimension is a state of consciousness where we experience life as multidimensional beings, recognizing the interconnectedness of all things. In this higher dimensional reality, the focus shifts away from the dualistic thinking of the third dimension—where everything is seen as good or bad, right or wrong—and moves toward an awareness of unity, love, and harmony. The fifth dimension is characterized by higher vibrational frequencies, where we live in alignment with our true essence as energy beings.

Shift from density to lightness—As we ascend into the fifth dimension, we let go of the densities that have weighed us down—emotional baggage, limiting beliefs, and old stories that keep us stuck in lower frequencies. In doing so, we become lighter, more expansive, and more aligned with the flow of life. This lightness enables us to access higher states of consciousness, where we experience greater clarity, peace, and joy.

Energy over form—In the fifth dimension, we understand that we are primarily energetic beings, and our physical bodies are just one aspect of our existence. By recognizing ourselves as energy, we tap into our ability to consciously create and shape our reality. We are no longer bound by the limitations of the third-dimensional experience, where we overly identify with the physical world and external circumstances.

Live in harmony with higher frequencies—The fifth dimension vibrates at a frequency of love, unity, and peace. As we align with these frequencies, we naturally experience more synchronicities, flow, and ease in our lives. Challenges may still arise, but from this higher perspective, we approach them with acceptance and wisdom, knowing that they serve our growth and evolution.

Choosing Your Timeline

One of the most empowering aspects of living in the fifth-dimensional experience is the realization that all timelines exist simultaneously. You can choose which timeline you want to experience based on your thoughts, emotions, and beliefs. By aligning yourself with the timeline that resonates with your highest self, you can create a reality that reflects love, abundance, and purpose.

In the fifth dimension, the concept of linear time dissolves. Instead of experiencing time as a progression of past, present, and future, we understand that all potential timelines exist in the present moment. This means that the version of reality you desire—whether it's one of greater success, fulfillment, or peace—already exists. By aligning your thoughts, feelings, and actions with that timeline, you shift into that reality.

To consciously choose your desired timeline, it's essential to hold the vision of the reality you want to experience. Visualize yourself already living in that timeline and feel the emotions associated with it—joy, love, gratitude, and abundance. The more you embody these feelings, the more you align your energy with that timeline. Your emotions are the energetic bridge between your current reality and your desired future.

Once you've aligned with a higher timeline, it's important to maintain your vibrational frequency to stay in that reality. This involves letting go of the old stories, beliefs, and habits that belong to lower dimensional timelines. You cannot carry the weight of your past into the new reality, as it will pull you back into old patterns. Instead, stay committed to your new vibration, knowing that you have the power to create and sustain the life you desire.

Allowing People and Situations to Fall Away

As you shift into a higher dimensional experience, you may find that certain people, relationships, or situations no longer resonate with your new frequency. While this can be challenging, it's important to honor the natural growth process and allow these changes to occur without resistance.

Outgrowing old relationships—As your vibration rises, you may notice that some relationships feel misaligned with your new reality. This is not a reflection of judgment or superiority, but rather an indication that you and the other person are on different paths. By allowing these relationships to fall away with love and compassion, you make space for new connections that resonate with your higher frequency.

Let go with love—It's natural to feel sadness or loss when people or situations leave your life, but letting go with love allows you to honor the lessons and experiences you shared. Recognize that every relationship has its purpose, and by releasing it, you are giving yourself and the other person the freedom to continue growing. Letting go with love ensures you remain aligned with your higher self and your chosen timeline.

Trust the process of alignment—Trust that as you align with higher frequencies, the universe will bring new people, opportunities, and experiences into your life that are in harmony with your vibration. By letting go of what no longer serves you, you open the door to new possibilities that reflect the timeline you are now choosing to live in.

Maintaining Your Higher Vibration

Living in the fifth-dimensional experience requires consistent attention to your vibrational frequency. As you navigate your daily life, it's important to remain conscious of the thoughts, emotions, and actions that either support or detract from your higher timeline.

Daily energy practices—To maintain your higher vibration, incorporate energy practices such as meditation, breathwork, or visualization into your daily routine. These practices help you stay grounded in love and peace while clearing any lower vibrational energies that may arise. Regularly tuning into your energy field ensures you remain aligned with the higher frequencies of the fifth dimension.

Mindful living—Practice mindful awareness in your thoughts, words, and actions. Notice when you are tempted to slip into old patterns of fear, judgment, or limitation, and gently bring your focus back to love and compassion. Mindfulness helps you stay present and aligned with your higher self, preventing you from being pulled back into lower dimensional timelines.

Surround yourself with higher vibrations—The people, environments, and activities you engage with influence your vibration. Surround yourself with supportive relationships, uplifting environments, and activities that nourish your soul. By intentionally choosing higher vibrational experiences, you reinforce your alignment with the fifth-dimensional reality and continue growing spiritually.

By aligning our thoughts, emotions, and actions with higher frequencies, we ascend to a reality reflecting love, peace, and unity.

Letting go of old stories, limiting beliefs, and relationships that no longer resonate is essential for staying in this new timeline. As we release what no longer serves us, we create space for new possibilities and experiences that align with our highest self.

In the next chapter, we will explore how to continue deepening your connection to the fifth-dimensional experience, learning to navigate challenges while maintaining your alignment with higher frequencies and living as a conscious creator of your reality.

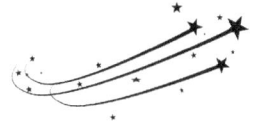

CHAPTER 20

DEEPENING YOUR CONNECTION TO THE FIFTH-DIMENSIONAL EXPERIENCE AND NAVIGATING CHALLENGES WITH HIGHER CONSCIOUSNESS

As you continue on your path of spiritual ascension, the journey into the fifth-dimensional experience deepens. Living in this higher dimensional state requires you to remain aligned with higher frequencies, even when challenges arise. The key to staying in the fifth dimension is learning how to navigate life from a place of conscious awareness, love, and trust rather than falling back into old patterns of fear, doubt, and judgment.

In this chapter, we will explore how to strengthen your connection to the fifth-dimensional experience, ensuring you maintain your alignment even in difficult moments. By living as a conscious creator of your reality, you can transform challenges into opportunities for growth and remain grounded in the higher vibrations of love, peace, and unity.

Strengthening Your Connection to the Fifth-Dimensional Experience

The fifth-dimensional experience is not a destination; it is a state of being that requires continuous nurturing and practice. To deepen your connection to this higher state, it's essential to maintain a conscious awareness of your thoughts, emotions, and actions, aligning them with the frequencies of love, compassion, and unity.

Tune into your higher self—Your higher self is your guide and connection to the fifth dimension. It is the aspect of you that operates from a place of infinite wisdom and love. To strengthen this connection, make it a daily practice to tune into your higher self through meditation, visualization, or simply quiet reflection. Ask for guidance, insight, or clarity when you need it, and trust that your higher self will lead you toward the best path for your growth.

Listen to your intuition—Your intuition is the voice of your higher self communicating with you in real time. By listening to and trusting your intuition, you align yourself with the fifth-dimensional flow. Pay attention to the subtle nudges, feelings, or insights that guide your decisions and actions. The more you trust this inner knowing, the stronger your connection to the higher dimensions becomes.

Live in alignment with love—The fifth-dimensional experience is rooted in unconditional love—for yourself, others, and the world. Make it a priority to align your thoughts and actions with love in every situation. When confronted with challenges, ask yourself, What would love do here? By choosing love, you stay grounded in the higher frequencies and contribute to expanding your consciousness.

Consistency in spiritual practice—Consistency is crucial to maintaining your higher vibration. Make it a habit to engage in daily spiritual practices that strengthen your connection to your higher self and the fifth-dimensional experience. These practices may include meditation, prayer, visualization, or journaling. The more consistently you engage with these practices, the more deeply you will stay aligned with higher frequencies.

Mindful living—Mindfulness is a powerful tool for staying connected to the present moment and maintaining awareness of your thoughts, emotions, and energy. By cultivating mindfulness in everything you do—whether working, interacting with others, or simply going about your daily tasks—you remain consciously aligned with your higher self. This helps you avoid slipping back into old patterns of fear or judgment and keeps you focused on creating a life that reflects your highest timeline.

Ground yourself in the physical world—While the fifth-dimensional experience is one of higher frequencies, it's important to stay grounded in the physical world as well. Engage in activities that connect you to the Earth and your body, such as spending time in nature, practicing yoga, or engaging in physical exercise. Grounding helps you balance life's spiritual and physical aspects, ensuring you remain present and rooted even as you ascend.

Navigating Challenges from a Higher Perspective

Even as we ascend into the fifth dimension, challenges will still arise. However, the way we respond to these challenges differs from how we might have reacted in the third dimension. In the fifth-dimensional experience, we see challenges as opportunities for growth and approach them with a sense of peace and trust rather than fear or resistance.

Shift your perspective on challenges—In the third-dimensional mindset, challenges are often viewed as obstacles or problems to overcome. However, from the perspective of the fifth dimension, challenges are seen as gifts for growth and expansion. Every difficult situation carries within it the seeds of transformation, helping you learn more about yourself, your emotions, and your spiritual path. When challenges arise, ask yourself, What is this teaching me? How can I grow from this? Shifting your perspective allows you to remain open to the lessons and opportunities present in every situation.

Stay grounded in higher frequencies during difficult times—When faced with a challenge, it's easy to slip back into lower vibrational states of fear, anxiety, or frustration. To stay grounded in the fifth-dimensional experience, consciously maintain your higher vibration. Take time to center yourself, breathe deeply, and connect with the higher frequencies of love and peace. Practices such as meditation, breathwork, or walking in nature can help you realign with your higher self and regain perspective.

Trust the process of life—One of the most important lessons of the fifth dimension is learning to trust the process of life. Even when things seem uncertain or difficult, trust that everything is unfolding in divine order for your highest good. Challenges are part of the natural flow of growth, and by trusting the process, you can navigate them with more grace and ease. Trust that your higher self and the universe are guiding you toward your highest timeline, even when the path seems unclear.

Choose to rise above lower frequencies—When faced with conflict or negativity, it's easy to get pulled back into lower vibrational states such as fear, anger, or frustration. However, as a conscious creator, you can choose how you respond. Practice consciously rising above these lower frequencies by responding from a place of love, compassion, and understanding. This allows you to maintain alignment with higher dimensions, even in the face of challenges.

Living as a Conscious Creator of Your Reality

In the fifth-dimensional experience, you are a conscious creator of your reality. This means that your thoughts, emotions, and actions constantly shape the world around you. By remaining mindful of your energy and aligning it with your highest intentions, you can actively co-create a reality that reflects your deepest desires and soul's purpose.

Take ownership of your thoughts and emotions—As a conscious creator, it's important to take full responsibility for the thoughts and emotions you are projecting into the world. Your energy is powerful, and every thought you think and emotion you feel contributes to the reality you experience. If you slip into negative thought patterns, gently bring your focus back to higher vibrations. Replace fear with trust, judgment with compassion, and doubt with faith.

Set clear intentions—Manifestation in the fifth dimension is driven by your intentions. Be clear about what you want to create, whether it's greater abundance, deeper relationships, or spiritual growth. Set your intentions from a place of love and alignment with your higher self, and trust that the universe will support you in bringing those intentions to life. Regularly revisit your intentions and affirm them through visualization, positive affirmations, or journaling.

Create from a place of alignment—The key to manifesting in the fifth dimension is to ensure that your creations come from a place of alignment with your true self. When your desires and intentions are in harmony with your soul's purpose, they are more likely to manifest easily and gracefully. Ask yourself if this desire comes from a place of love and authenticity. Does it align with your higher self? By creating from a place of alignment, you ensure that what you manifest is in your highest good.

Integrating Fifth-Dimensional Living Into All Aspects of Your Life

As you continue to deepen your connection to the fifth-dimensional experience, it's important to integrate this higher consciousness into all areas of your life—your relationships, work, health, and personal growth. By embodying the principles of love, compassion, and unity in every aspect of your life, you become a living example of fifth-dimensional living.

Live with purpose—A key aspect of fifth-dimensional living is aligning your actions with your soul's purpose. This means making choices that reflect your true values and contribute to your spiritual growth. Whether it's through your career, relationships, or personal projects, ensure that what you're doing is in harmony with your highest self. When you live with purpose, you create a sense of fulfillment and joy that sustains you on your spiritual journey.

Engage with the physical world mindfully—While it's important to remain connected to higher frequencies, engaging fully with the physical world is also essential. This means being present in your interactions with others, enjoying the pleasures of the material world, and taking care of your physical body. The fifth-dimensional experience isn't about escaping the physical world but bringing higher consciousness into everything you do. By engaging mindfully with the physical world, you integrate the spiritual into the everyday.

Balance self-care and service—Fifth-dimensional living is about personal growth and contributing to the greater good. Finding a balance between self-care, nurturing your energy and well-being, service to others, and offering your gifts and love to the world is important. By balancing these two aspects, you create a life that is both fulfilling and aligned with the principles of love and unity.

Bring higher consciousness into relationships—In your relationships, practice nonjudgment, acceptance, and compassion. Recognize that everyone is on their unique soul journey, and approach your interactions from a place of love and understanding. By holding space for others to grow at their own pace, you foster deeper connections and create relationships based on mutual respect and authenticity.

Align your work with your higher self—Whether in your career or personal projects, align your work with your soul's purpose. Ask yourself, *Does this work reflect my true values? Does it contribute to the collective* *good?* When your work aligns with your higher self, you experience more fulfillment and joy in your endeavors. Trust that by following your passion and purpose, you are contributing to the greater evolution of consciousness.

Maintain balance and harmony—Fifth-dimensional living is about maintaining balance and harmony in all areas of life. Prioritize your well-being—physically, emotionally, mentally, and spiritually. Take time to care for your body, mind, and soul through regular self-care practices. By staying balanced and harmonious within yourself, you ensure that you remain aligned with the higher frequencies of the fifth dimension.

Building Resilience for Long-Term Growth

Sustaining your connection to the fifth-dimensional experience requires resilience—the ability to bounce back from challenges, adapt to change, and continue evolving spiritually. Building resilience ensures you can maintain your alignment with higher frequencies, even in the face of obstacles or setbacks.

Practice self-compassion—One of the most important aspects of building resilience is practicing self-compassion. Be gentle with yourself, especially during difficult times. Remember that spiritual growth is a journey, and it's normal to experience ups and downs along the way. When you make a mistake or face a setback, approach yourself with kindness and understanding, knowing that each experience is an opportunity for growth.

Adapt to change—The spiritual journey is constantly evolving, and so are you. It's important to stay open to change and adaptable in your approach to life. As you grow spiritually, you may find that your beliefs, relationships, or priorities shift. Embrace these changes as part of your evolution, and trust that each shift is leading you closer to your highest self. By remaining flexible and open, you build resilience for long-term growth.

Trust your inner guidance—To sustain your connection to higher dimensions, it's essential to develop a deep sense of trust in your inner guidance. Your higher self always guides you toward your highest path, even when the way forward seems unclear. Cultivate a strong connection to your intuition and trust that it's leading you in the right direction. This trust will give you the resilience to navigate any challenge confidently and gracefully.

Thriving in Higher Dimensions with Joy and Fulfillment

Living in alignment with the fifth-dimensional experience brings not only spiritual growth but also a deep sense of joy and fulfillment. By sustaining your connection to higher frequencies, you create a life that reflects your highest potential and allows you to thrive in all areas of your existence.

Cultivate joy as a spiritual practice—Joy is a natural expression of living in alignment with higher dimensions. Make it a point to cultivate joy in your daily life, whether through creative expression, connection with others, or simply appreciating the beauty around you. Joy is a high-vibrational frequency that amplifies your connection to the fifth dimension and enhances your overall well-being.

Celebrate your growth—As you continue to evolve spiritually, celebrate your growth. Acknowledge the progress you've made, the lessons you've learned, and the challenges you've overcome. By celebrating your journey, you reinforce your alignment with higher frequencies and create space for even more growth and expansion.

Thrive in alignment with your highest self—When you sustain your connection to higher dimensions over the long term, you naturally thrive in all areas of your life. Your relationships become more authentic and fulfilling, your work aligns with your soul's purpose, and your inner world reflects peace, love, and joy. Thriving in alignment with your higher self allows you to live a grounded and spiritually expansive life.

By living as a conscious creator of your reality, you can transform obstacles into opportunities for growth and remain aligned with the vibrations of love, peace, and unity. Maintaining higher frequencies in daily life requires consistent mindfulness, energy practices, and intentional alignment with your higher self. By integrating these principles into all aspects of your life, you embody the fifth-dimensional experience and contribute to the collective awakening of humanity.

By building a strong foundation of daily spiritual practices, navigating challenges with resilience, and balancing the spiritual with the physical, you create a life that reflects your highest self and contributes to the collective evolution of humanity.

As you maintain your connection to higher frequencies, you live as a conscious creator, transforming challenges into opportunities for growth and embodying the principles of love, compassion, and unity. This path not only brings fulfillment to your life but also elevates the consciousness of the world around you.

In the next chapter, we will reflect on the transformative power of living in alignment with the fifth-dimensional experience and how this journey not only enhances your own life but also contributes to the collective awakening of humanity.

CHAPTER 21

CO-CREATING
A NEW REALITY THROUGH
FIFTH-DIMENSIONAL LIVING

As we come to the end of this journey, it is time to reflect on the profound transformative power of living in alignment with the fifth-dimensional experience. When you consciously choose to align with higher frequencies of love, unity, and peace, you transform your life and contribute to humanity's collective awakening. Together, we are co-creating a new reality based on the principles of love, unity, and higher consciousness.

This chapter will explore how your personal transformation through fifth-dimensional living becomes a powerful catalyst for collective change. By living as an example of higher consciousness, you inspire others to awaken to their potential, contributing to a ripple effect that accelerates humanity's evolution toward greater unity and oneness. This journey of spiritual growth and alignment is not just about individual awakening but co-creating a new Earth where love and unity are the foundation of our shared experience.

The Transformative Power of Living in Alignment with the Fifth Dimension

Living in alignment with the fifth dimension fundamentally shifts every aspect of your life. As you embrace higher vibrations and let go of limiting beliefs, fear, and judgment, you create a reality reflecting the love, joy, and peace of the higher dimensions. This personal transformation extends far beyond individual change—it sets the stage for collective evolution.

When you align with the fifth dimension, you experience life as a natural flow of synchronicities, abundance, and ease. Challenges are met with trust and an opportunity for growth rather than resistance or fear. You live in a state of greater awareness, recognizing the interconnectedness of all things. Your thoughts, emotions, and actions align with your soul's purpose, and you naturally attract experiences that support your growth and fulfillment.

As you live in higher dimensions, your consciousness expands to include a greater understanding of yourself and the world around you. You begin to see beyond the physical realm, recognizing that you are a multidimensional being with access to infinite potential. This expanded awareness allows you to live with more clarity, purpose, and wisdom as you understand that your reality reflects your inner state.

The fifth-dimensional experience is rooted in unconditional love. As you align with these higher frequencies, you naturally embody love and compassion in your interactions with others. You become a living example of the power of love to heal, transform, and uplift. By embodying these qualities, you inspire others to embrace love and compassion in their lives, creating a ripple effect of positive change.

The Ripple Effect: How Your Transformation Inspires Others

One of the most beautiful aspects of living in alignment with the fifth dimension is the ripple effect it creates. As you transform your life, you become a beacon of light for others. Your higher vibration influences those around you, encouraging them to awaken to their potential and begin their journey of spiritual evolution.

Inspire through example—Your personal transformation is a powerful example to others. By living authentically, aligning with love and unity, and embracing higher consciousness, you show others what is possible. People are naturally drawn to your light and may seek to understand how you have cultivated such peace, joy, and fulfillment. By aligning with your highest self, you inspire others to explore their spiritual path and make positive changes in their lives.

Elevate collective consciousness—Every time you raise your vibration, you contribute to the collective elevation of humanity's consciousness. As more individuals awaken and align with higher frequencies, the collective energy of the planet shifts. This creates a ripple effect that accelerates the spiritual awakening of humanity as a whole. Your personal growth and alignment help to raise the vibration of the entire planet, contributing to the collective evolution of consciousness.

Create space for unity and oneness—By embodying the principles of love, compassion, and unity, you create space for others to experience the same. You hold a higher frequency that others can resonate with, allowing them to feel more connected, understood, and accepted. This sense of oneness fosters a deeper connection among all beings, helping to dissolve the illusion of separation that has long characterized the third-dimensional experience.

Co-Creating a New Reality

As more and more individuals align with the fifth-dimensional experience, we collectively begin to co-create a new reality. This new Earth is not something that exists in the distant future—it is a reality that we are actively creating in the present moment through our thoughts, beliefs, and actions. The more we embody higher consciousness, the more we bring forth a world grounded in love, unity, and higher awareness.

Live from a place of unity consciousness—The new reality we are co-creating is one where unity consciousness prevails. In this reality, we understand that we are all connected; we are all expressions of the same Source energy. We no longer see others as separate from ourselves but as unique reflections of the divine. This unity consciousness leads to a world where cooperation, compassion, and mutual support are the foundation of our interactions, both personally and globally.

Manifest a reality based on love—In the fifth dimension, love drives everything we create. As more individuals align with higher vibrations, we collectively manifest a reality that reflects unconditional love, compassion, and peace. This new reality is one where fear, judgment, and division are replaced by understanding, acceptance, and unity. The world we are co-creating is one where every being is honored and valued for their unique contribution to the whole.

Build a future of abundance and harmony—The fifth-dimensional experience is one of abundance and harmony. As we continue to co-create this new reality, we shift away from the old paradigms of scarcity, competition, and conflict. Instead, we build systems and structures that support the well-being of all beings and the planet itself. This future is one where resources are shared, creativity is nurtured, and every individual is empowered to live in alignment with their highest potential.

Your Role in the Collective Awakening

As we reflect on the journey of spiritual ascension and fifth-dimensional living, it's important to remember that you play an essential role in the collective awakening. Every choice you make to live in alignment with higher frequencies contributes to the greater transformation of humanity. Your willingness to embody love, compassion, and unity helps to create a brighter future for all beings.

Awaken others through your presence—Simply by aligning with your higher self, you awaken others to their potential. You don't need to force change or preach your beliefs—your presence alone is enough to inspire transformation. As you walk through the world as a beacon of light, others will feel your energy and be uplifted by it. Trust that by embodying higher consciousness, you are already contributing to the awakening of humanity.

Hold space for collective evolution—As humanity continues to evolve, there will be moments of turbulence and transition. It's important to hold space for this collective process, trusting that each challenge is a catalyst for greater growth. By staying grounded in your higher self and maintaining your alignment with love and unity, you help to anchor these higher frequencies on the planet. Your presence creates stability and support for others as they navigate their own awakening journey.

Contribute to the global shift—The shift to a higher dimensional reality is a global movement, and your role is integral to its success. As more people awaken and align with higher frequencies, the momentum of this shift accelerates. By living as a conscious creator, you are actively contributing to this global transformation, helping usher in a new era of peace, love, and unity on Earth.

Together, we are co-creating a new reality based on love, unity, and higher consciousness. By embracing your role as a conscious creator, you play a vital part in elevating the collective vibration and creating a new world where love and compassion are the foundation of our shared experience. The journey of spiritual ascension is not just a personal one—it is a journey that impacts the entire planet. As you continue to live in alignment with your higher self, trust that you are helping to create a brighter future for all.

Together, we are shaping the future of our planet—one that reflects the highest potential of all beings, where love reigns supreme and we all thrive in harmony.

In the final chapter, you will be led through an exercise to create and manifest your fifth-dimensional timeline reality.

CHAPTER 22

WHAT TIMELINE DO YOU CHOOSE?

Now that you understand the infinite nature of timelines and your ability to actively shift to the timeline you consciously choose, it's time to take inspired action. I strongly encourage you to take some time to fulfill this timeline exercise. You have nothing to lose and everything to gain in your life. It's time to Awaken to Your Multidimensional Self!

Exercise: Creating and Manifesting Your Fifth-Dimensional Timeline

In this exercise, you'll tap into the fifth-dimensional energy—a state of higher consciousness where love, unity, and abundance are the dominant frequencies—to create your desired timeline. This process will help you align your thoughts, feelings, and energy with the reality you want to manifest, drawing you closer to your highest timeline.

Step 1: Setting Your Intention

To begin, find a quiet space where you won't be disturbed. Sit comfortably, close your eyes, and take a few deep breaths. Allow yourself to relax and let go of any tension in your body. Bring your awareness fully into the present moment.

- **Visualize your desired timeline**—Imagine the version of your life you want to experience. This is your fifth-dimensional timeline, a reality where you live in alignment with your highest self. What does it look like? How do you feel?

- **Ask yourself**—What are the core desires you wish to manifest in this timeline? Is it financial abundance, deep love, inner peace, fulfilling work, or vibrant health? Be specific in your vision. The more clarity you have, the easier it will be to align with this timeline.

Once you have a clear picture, set your intention by writing down what you want to manifest on a piece of paper or in a journal. Begin with: "In my fifth-dimensional timeline, I experience …"

For example:

- "In my fifth-dimensional timeline, I experience joy, peace, and love in every area of my life."

- "In my fifth-dimensional timeline, I am financially abundant and use my resources to uplift others."

- "In my fifth-dimensional timeline, I am in perfect health, full of vitality, and deeply connected to my body."

Step 2: Connect with the Feeling of Your Desired Timeline

Now that you've clarified your vision, it's time to embody the energy of this timeline.

- **Visualize** your future self in this timeline. How does it feel to live in this reality? Close your eyes and imagine waking up in the morning, going through your day as if you're already living in this higher dimensional state.

- **Embrace the emotions**—Feel the joy, peace, excitement, and love of this new reality. Allow those feelings to fill your heart and radiate throughout your body. The key to manifesting from a higher dimension is aligning your energy with the vibration of your desires. In this case, the feelings of abundance, love, and harmony must be present in your emotional field.

If it's challenging to tap into those emotions at first, try asking yourself:

- How would I feel if this timeline were already my reality?
- What would I think, believe, or say to myself?
- How would my interactions with others change?

Step 3: Identify and Release Resistance

Now, bring your awareness to any limiting beliefs or self-doubts that may arise. These are often blocks that prevent you from fully stepping into your desired timeline.

- **Identify resistance**—Write down any thoughts or fears that come up. Common limiting beliefs might include, "I don't deserve this," "This is too good to be true," or "I'm not capable of achieving this." Recognizing these beliefs is crucial because they are the resistance keeping you from your fifth-dimensional timeline.
- **Release and reframe**—Once you've identified the resistance, challenge it. Replace each limiting belief with a positive affirmation that aligns with your desired reality. For example, if the limiting belief is "I'm not deserving," you could reframe it as "I am worthy of receiving abundance, love, and joy in every form."

Repeat your new affirmations several times, letting them sink into your subconscious mind.

Step 4: Shift Your Energy to Match the Fifth-Dimensional Frequency

In the fifth dimension, everything is vibrational. To attract your desired timeline, you must vibrate at the frequency of the reality you wish to experience. Here's how you can do this:

- **Meditate daily**—Spend 5-10 minutes each day in quiet meditation, focusing on the feelings of joy, love, and gratitude that come with your desired timeline. The more you connect with these emotions, the more you'll attract experiences that match this vibration.

- **Practice gratitude**—Begin each day with a gratitude practice. As you wake up, mentally list three things you're grateful for in your current life and three things you're grateful for in your desired timeline (even if they haven't manifested yet). Gratitude for the future as if it's already present is a powerful way to collapse timelines and bring your desires into reality.

- **Act as if**—Throughout the day, consciously act as though you are already living in your fifth-dimensional timeline. How would your future self behave? What choices would you make? Align your actions, decisions, and behaviors with the reality you are creating.

Step 5: Let Go and Trust

Once you have aligned yourself with your desired timeline, it's important to let go of attachment. Trust that the universe is working in your favor to bring this reality into existence. Remember, the fifth dimension operates on the frequency of flow and trust—not force or control.

- **Release control**—You don't need to micromanage how or when your manifestation will come. Instead, stay open to the process and know that the universe is rearranging everything to bring your desires to fruition.

- **Stay present**—Practice mindfulness and live fully in the present moment. Your current experience is part of the unfolding of your higher timeline, so embrace the journey with patience and trust.

Step 6: Take Inspired Action

The fifth dimension is about co-creation. While visualizing and raising your vibration are essential, taking inspired action is what moves you closer to your desired timeline.

- **Listen to your intuition**—Pay attention to nudges, ideas, or opportunities that come your way. These are signs guiding you toward your manifestation. Take small steps toward your goals every day, knowing that each action brings you closer to your desired timeline.

- **Stay aligned with your vision**—Ensure your actions are consistent with the timeline you want to create. For example, if you're manifesting financial abundance, take actions that demonstrate trust in that abundance, such as budgeting wisely, investing in yourself, or supporting others.

Step 7: Affirm and Reinforce

To strengthen your alignment with your desired timeline, use daily affirmations or mantras to keep your energy focused. Here are a few examples you can use:

- "I am aligned with my highest timeline, and everything I desire is flowing to me easily."

- "I am worthy of all the love, abundance, and joy the universe has to offer."

- "I trust the process and know that my desired reality is already on its way."

Repeat these affirmations multiple times throughout the day, especially when you feel doubt creeping in.

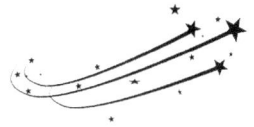

CONCLUSION

By following this exercise, you're not just visualizing your desired fifth-dimensional timeline, you're embodying it, raising your vibration, and aligning yourself with the energy of your dreams. With consistent practice, trust, and action, you'll find that your desired reality begins to manifest effortlessly, bringing you closer to a life filled with love, abundance, and fulfillment.

Thank you for embarking on this journey of higher consciousness and spiritual evolution. The path ahead is filled with infinite possibilities, and by living in alignment with the fifth dimension, you are contributing to the collective awakening of humanity and the co-creation of a world based on love, peace, and unity.

Stay committed to the process, trust in the power of your own vibration, and know that you can manifest any timeline you choose.

ABOUT THE AUTHOR

Dr. Lisa Thompson is an internationally recognized best-selling author, speaker, Galactic Ambassador, and intuitive transformational coach bridging the realms of science and spirituality. As a lifelong experiencer of extraterrestrial contact, she has established herself as a multidimensional channeler, communicating with 13 higher dimensional ET races, primarily the Arcturian Uluru. Lisa is dedicated to empowering individuals to step into their higher purpose by embracing self-love, trusting their intuition, and taking inspired action to overcome fear.

With a PhD in Organismal Biology and Anatomy from the University of Chicago, Lisa's expertise in evolutionary biology adds depth to her work. Her academic background provides a solid foundation for her exploration of galactic wisdom, making her a leader in merging scientific rigor with spiritual awareness. Her insights into the embodiment of ancient human DNA blend with metaphysical teachings to offer a transformative perspective on humanity's path toward global awakening and ascension.

Lisa is the best-selling author of several books that integrate cosmic wisdom with practical guidance, including:

- *Wisdom of the Galactics: Channeled Messages to Elevate Your Life*
- *Connection to the Cosmos: Remembering Your Galactic Heritage and Embracing Your Oneness*

- *Sacred Soul Love: Manifesting True Love and Happiness by Revealing and Healing Blockages and Limitations*
- *Sacred Soul Spaces: Designing Your Personal Oasis*

Her reputation as an inspiring speaker has led her to prominent stages at spiritual and metaphysical summits worldwide. Her weekly podcast, **Connection to the Cosmos with Dr. Lisa Thompson**, is a trusted resource for spiritual seekers, exploring topics like galactic heritage, ET contact, metaphysical science, channeling, spiritual awakening, and human consciousness evolution.

As a multidimensional Starseed, Lisa teaches humanity about love, unity, and our cosmic interconnection. She has experienced direct contact with several ET races, including the Arcturians, Pleiadians, and Sirians, and channels their wisdom to guide Earth's spiritual evolution. These authentic experiences offer unique insights into humanity's role in the universe and our journey toward ascension.

Lisa also offers **Big Island UFO Tours** in Hawaii, where participants witness UFO phenomena and deepen their connection to the cosmic family through stargazing. As a channeler and Advanced Certified Past/Parallel Life Regression Coach, she uses tools like Human Design, Sound Healing, and her unique **Galactic Ascension Channeling** modality to help individuals release trauma and live more expansive lives.

She has created ten oracle card decks, leads retreats in Hawaii, and teaches online classes. For more information, visit **www.DrLisaJThompson. com**.

STAY CONNECTED WITH DR. LISA

You can connect with Lisa online and via social media here:

Websites:

www.DrLisaJThompson.com—sign up for her email list!

www.BigIslandUFOTours.com

Facebook:

www.facebook.com/DrLisaThompsonAuthor

www.facebook.com/BigIslandUFOTours

www.facebook.com/groups/sacredsoulspaces

www.facebook.com/groups/connectiontothecosmos

Instagram:

www.instagram.com/drlisathompson_author/

YouTube:

Connection to the Cosmos with Dr. Lisa Thompson